Rising Stars Reading Planet

Galaxy

NINA FILIPEK

Yellow

Blue

Green

Orange

Teacher's Guide E

Although every effort has been made to ensure that website addresses are correct at time of going to press, Rising Stars cannot be held responsible for the content of any website mentioned in this book. It is sometimes possible to find a relocated web page by typing in the address of the home page for a website in the URL window of your browser.

Hachette UK's policy is to use papers that are natural, renewable and recyclable products and made from wood grown in sustainable forests. The logging and manufacturing processes are expected to conform to the environmental regulations of the country of origin.

Orders: please contact Bookpoint Ltd, 130 Park Drive, Milton Park, Abingdon, Oxon OX14 4SE. Telephone: (44) 01235 400555. Email primary@bookpoint.co.uk. Lines are open from 9 a.m. to 5 p.m., Monday to Saturday, with a 24-hour message answering service. Visit our website at www.risingstars-uk.com for details of the full range of Rising Stars publications.

Online support and queries email: onlinesupport@risingstars-uk.com

ISBN: 978 1 51043373 1

Text, design and layout © 2018 Rising Stars UK Ltd
First published in 2018 by Rising Stars UK Ltd
Rising Stars UK Ltd, part of Hodder Education Group
An Hachette UK Company
Carmelite House, 50 Victoria Embankment, London EC4Y 0DZ
www.risingstars-uk.com
All facts are correct at time of going to press.

Impression number 10 9 8 7 6 5 4 3 2 1
Year 2022 2021 2020 2019 2018

Author: Nina Filipek
Publisher: Helen Parker
Commissioning Editor: Becca Law
Development Editors: Catherine Allison, Rebecca Hamway
Line artwork: Marek Jagucki
Academic Consultant: Professor Clare Wood, Coventry University
Educational Consultants: Madeleine Barnes, Helen Marron and Abigail Steel
Brand design: Amparo Barrera, Kneath Associates
Cover design: Julie Martin
Text design: Lorraine Inglis
Book design: Sarah Garbett @ Sg Creative Services
Editorial: Sarah Davies and Hamish Baxter

Acknowledgements
The Quack in the Kitchen, illustrated by Catalina Echeverri/Plum Pudding Illustration, p26 © Milos Luzanin/Shutterstock, p26 © Jesus Cervantes/Shutterstock, *The Magic Paintbox*, illustrated by James Mayhew/The Ben Illis Agency, p35 © Matyas Rehak/Shutterstock, *Into the Woods*, illustrated by Dan Widdowson/Bright Group International, Richard and the Lions, illustrated by Giovanni Pota/Astound US, *The Jumpy Bumpy Feeling*, illustrated by Anna-Lena Keuhler/Plum Pudding Illustration

All rights reserved. Apart from any use permitted under UK copyright law, the material in this publication is copyright and cannot be photocopied or otherwise produced in its entirety or copied onto acetate without permission. Electronic copying is not permitted. Permission is given to teachers to make copies of photocopiable masters, which are clearly marked at the bottom of each page, for classroom distribution only, to pupils within their own school or educational institution. The material may not be copied in unlimited quantities, kept on behalf of others, distributed outside the purchasing institution, copied onwards, sold to third parties, or stored for future use in a retrieval system. This permission is subject to the payment of the purchase price of the book. If you wish to use the material in any way other than as specified you must apply in writing to the Publisher at the above address.

A catalogue record for this title is available from the British Library.

CONTENTS

Introduction

- Welcome to *Rising Stars Reading Planet* — 4
- An introduction to *Rising Stars Reading Planet Galaxy* — 6
- The science behind speech rhythm activities — 7
- Guided and independent reading — 10
- *Galaxy* book bands/levels — 12
- Session focus ideas — 13
- Engaging parents with children's reading — 14
- Meeting National Curriculum requirements — 16
- IPA chart — 18
- Phonics progression mapping/alignment — 19

Teaching notes

- The Quack in the Kitchen — 20
- Be a Good Friend — 22
- Get to the Airport — 24
- Teddy Bears — 26
- The String — 28
- Picture a Sunset — 30
- The Magic Paintbox — 32
- Into the Woods — 34
- Catch Up, Koala! — 36
- Amazing Animation — 38
- Vanya the Viking — 40
- Play Outside — 42
- Rumpelstiltskin — 44
- Toys From 100 Years Ago — 46
- Sophie Goes to the Ballet — 48
- My Super Senses — 50
- Billy Builds Something Big — 52
- My Nature Activity Book — 54
- Robin Hood and the Golden Arrow — 56
- Incredible Creatures from Greek Myths — 58
- The Samurai's Brave Daughter — 60
- Richard and the Lions — 62
- The Jumpy Bumpy Feeling — 64
- Laugh Out Loud — 66

Assessment and tracking

- *Galaxy* assessment guidance — 68
- Tracking and monitoring sheets — 70
- Using a running record for assessment — 76

Welcome to *Rising Stars Reading Planet*

What is *Reading Planet*?

Rising Stars Reading Planet is an extensive and exciting reading scheme for Reception and Key Stage 1 providing carefully graded readers that are also 'real books' to help children develop a lifelong love of reading as they learn.

An experienced team of education experts – children's authors, editors and consultants – has created these books for you so that you can simply enjoy the experience of teaching children to read.

The *Reading Planet* scheme contains inbuilt progression that helps children meet age-related expectations for reading. *Reading Planet* has been developed using findings from the latest research to get children reading-ready, embed phonics, deepen comprehension and get children hooked on reading. The scheme is made up of four strands to ensure you have a fantastic variety and choice of books at every reading level.

A unique Lilac strand uses a powerful combination of speech rhythm sensitivity activities, wordless picture books and first word books to help children develop essential early language skills for reading readiness.

Fully decodable phonics books that allow children to practise their phonics skills in context, develop emerging reading skills and gradually improve their skills in decoding words of increasing complexity.

Follow the adventures of Rav, Asha, Tess, Finn and Stefan – five of the residents of Comet Street. Exciting stories featuring a cast of fun and feisty characters that children will love to go on adventures with.

A wonderful collection of fiction, non-fiction, poetry and plays to capture the interest of every child and help to develop a lifelong love of reading.

All of the *Reading Planet* books are levelled according to book-banding conventions, enabling you easily to match appropriate books to the reading abilities of the children in your school.

READING PLANET GALAXY

Every book comes with comprehensive cover notes to support children during one-on-one reading sessions. Here is an example from the *Galaxy* strand:

In this book
A list of tricky words that the child might need extra support with while reading.

Before reading
Suggested starting points including questions to help the child engage with the book cover and title.

After reading
Practical follow-up activities and discussion points to help develop understanding.

Reading tip
Tips for getting children 'reading-ready'.

Ready-to-read activity
Simple/practical activities based on the latest research findings into how children learn to read most effectively.

While reading
Practical ideas and example questions for the adult to use while sharing the book.

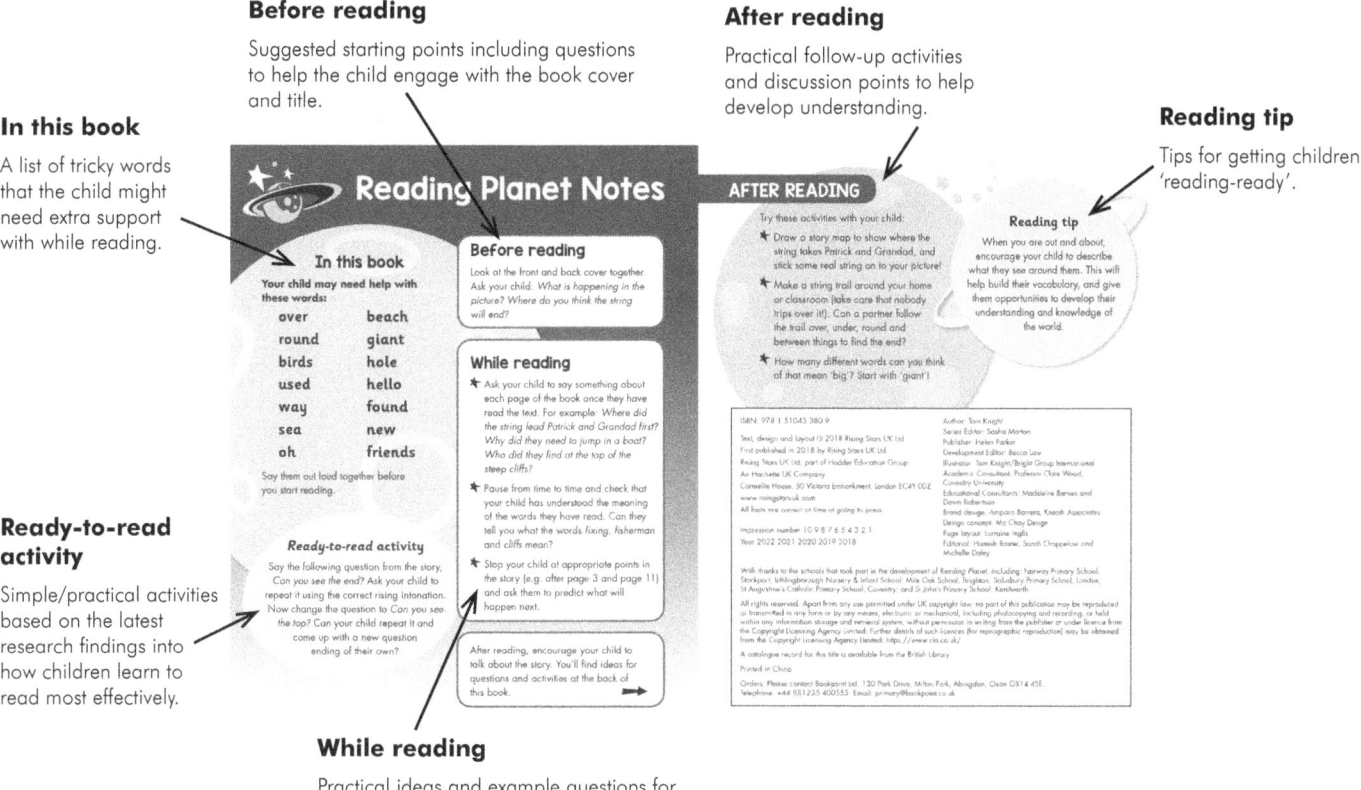

Each strand also comes with Teacher Guides that have been created in line with current best teaching practice and using the latest evidence-based research. Packed full of useful guidance, lesson plans and activity ideas, the Teacher Guides are a fantastic source of teaching inspiration and support guided group reading sessions within the classroom. Here is an example from the *Galaxy* strand:

A helpful list of ideas to try after reading, including further comprehension questions and follow-up activities.

Guided group reading session notes to use before, during and after reading in the classroom.

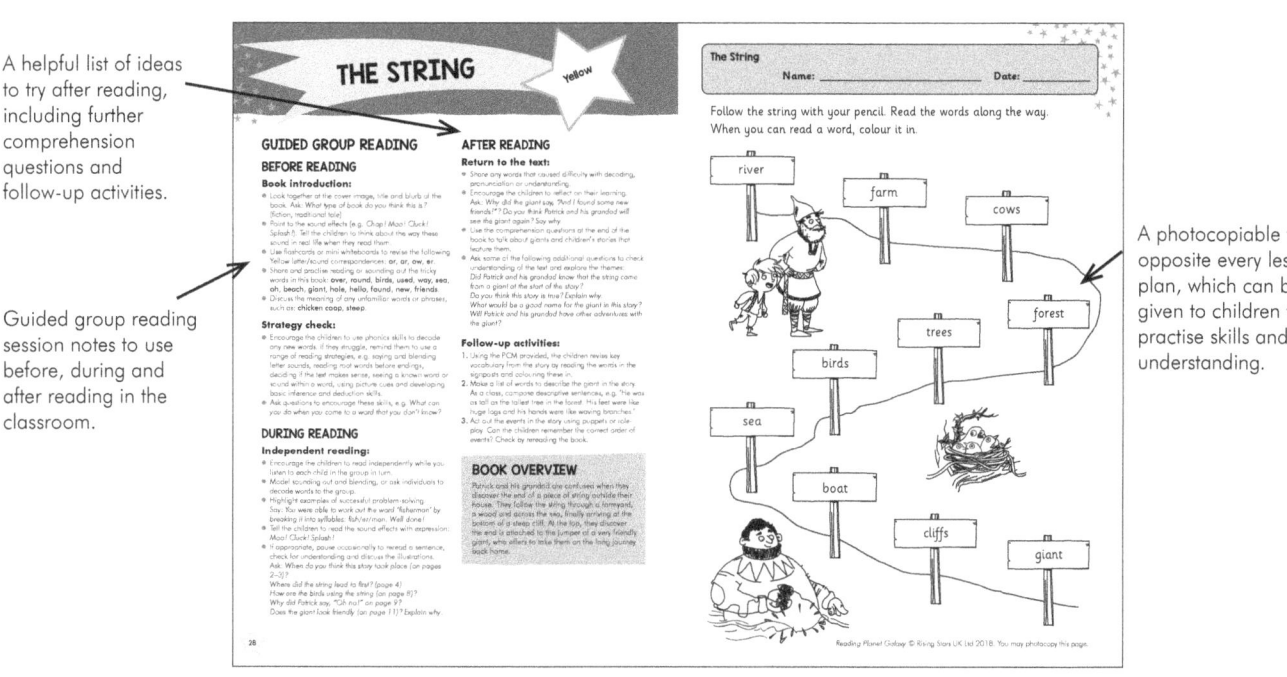

A photocopiable worksheet opposite every lesson plan, which can be given to children to help practise skills and secure understanding.

The Teacher Guides also include assessment and tracking grids to help you monitor the impact of *Reading Planet*.

We hope you enjoy exploring *Reading Planet* with your children as much as we have enjoyed creating it! Be sure to check our website for helpful blog posts, free resources and our latest news.

An introduction to *Rising Stars Reading Planet Galaxy*

What types of books are included within *Galaxy*?

There are a wide variety of genres and categories of book within the *Reading Planet Galaxy* strand to provide readers with a wealth of choice. As well as featuring decodable words appropriate to book band levels, the *Galaxy* books include specific topic words to widen children's vocabulary while they read.

There is also a range of both fiction and non-fiction titles within the *Galaxy* strand, covering plenty of topics and themes to capture the interest of every child and help to develop a life-long love of reading.

Why is it important to provide fiction and non-fiction?

Fiction books are good for:

- developing readers' feelings, emotions and perceptions of characters and situations
- building reading skills linked to creativity, passion and experiences
- unlocking many academic and social benefits for children learning to read: for a young reader wrapped up in a story, the characters represent real people facing real problems in the real world, and the credibility of characters holds the children's interest and creates an emotional investment in the reading process
- providing role models through the characters who can help children to develop the ability to empathise with others.

Non-fiction books are good for:

- developing readers' knowledge and understanding of the world around them
- building skills that are linked to functional reading later in life, e.g. reading newspapers, instructions and work reports
- encouraging slower and more accurate word level reading, whereas fictional texts can be read with an element of speed and less accuracy as the reader picks up the meaning with pace and flow
- helping children learn to navigate and access textbooks in other subjects, preparing them for KS3 and beyond
- creating a positive impact on children's later writing abilities; as children grow older the required content of their writing will more often be based on non-fiction text types therefore acquiring early verbal and reading skills in areas such as explanation, instruction and recount is an advantage from an early age.

The science behind speech rhythm activities

Reading Planet is underpinned by the latest research into literacy development from Coventry University, and others. It embeds speech rhythm sensitivity training that is proven to directly impact on children's ability to master phonics and learn to read.

What is speech rhythm sensitivity?

Speech rhythm sensitivity is the ability to perceive aspects of spoken English, such as stress, intonation and timing, as well as the natural rhythm of language. It can be enhanced with simple but highly effective speech rhythm activities in the classroom.

What does the research say about speech rhythm?

Children who struggle to acquire reading skills can find speech processing challenging. This is linked to their natural ability to 'tune in' to the linguistic rhythms found in their mother tongue. Research has shown that developing sensitivity to these rhythmic elements of spoken language can positively impact reading acquisition, reading comprehension and also reduce reading difficulties:

- Thomson, Leong and Goswami (2013) conducted a comparison study using intervention programmes with a group of dyslexic children with a mean age of 9 years. The rhythmic intervention involved both speech rhythm and non-speech rhythm tasks, together with drumming exercises and computer-based activities. Results demonstrated the potential of rhythmic-based activities to enhance various literacy skills.

- In a similar study, Bhide, Power and Goswami (2013) further investigated the potential of rhythmic-based training with a group of poor readers aged 6–7 years. In this intervention, children's rhythmic awareness was trained through the application of tapping exercises, same-different judgement tasks on tempo and rhythm, clapping to a beat, rise-time discrimination and answering questions on the rhythm of a poem. Results were supportive of rhythmic-based training improving reading skills in dyslexic individuals and poor readers.

- Harrison et al (in preparation) conducted a further study focusing on a sample of beginner readers aged 4–5 years and struggling readers aged 7–8. Results illustrated that rhythmic-based intervention was effective for beginner readers as well as those who have already received some formal reading tuition.

Why include speech rhythm activities in a reading scheme?

Linking back to the idea that some children may struggle to 'tune in' to the linguistic rhythms of their mother tongue, and that this may be linked to later reading difficulties, it is vital to support children at the earliest possible opportunity.

Although *Reading Planet* has been developed with the National Curriculum in mind, where possible we have tried to include a range of speech rhythm activities.

Reading Planet's variety of activities encourages the development of rhythm-based skills both at home and school. This lays a solid foundation for children to become confident and able readers with a lifelong love of reading.

What activities are included in Yellow–Orange bands?

We have included a bank of speech rhythm activities to use with the Yellow–Orange *Galaxy* books. These activities can be used to develop stress, intonation, rhythm and timing skills. The example activities show how the activities can be linked to the *Galaxy* reading books and provide opportunities for children to respond to and produce rhythms, and develop their awareness of speech rhythm across a range of engaging themes and settings. As seen in the lower book bands, activities use a mixture of speech (voice) and non-speech (musical) activities as well as both speaking (productive) and listening (receptive) skills. At this level, as children are developing their reading fluency and comprehension, the focus moves more towards aspects of speech rhythm such as the use of stress to convey additional meaning (such as dragging out a syllable for effect).

See pages 8–9 for a full bank of speech rhythm activities to try.

References

Bhide, A., Power, A., and Goswami, U. (2013). 'A rhythmic musical intervention for poor readers: A comparison of efficacy with a letter-based intervention'. *Mind, Brain and Education*, 7 (2), 113–123.

Harrison, E., Wood, C., Holliman, A. J. and Vousden, J. 2018. 'The immediate and longer-term effectiveness of a speech-rhythm-based reading intervention for beginning readers'. Journal of Research in Reading, 41, 220–241.

Thomson, J. M., Leong, V., and Goswami, U. (2013). 'Auditory processing interventions and developmental dyslexia: A comparison of phonemic and rhythmic approaches'. *Reading and Writing*, 26 (2), 139–161.

Bank of speech rhythm activities

Here is a range of suggested speech rhythm activities that you can use with the reading books included in this guide, with examples of how they can be applied to specific books. They can be used to develop and assess children's sensitivity to speech rhythm.

Activity	Description	Children's response
Tap or clap to a beat	Use words or phrases from one of the books to tap a beat or rhythm. Can the children copy it? You can focus on differing rhythms, such as 'strong, weak, strong, weak' in comparison to 'strong, strong, weak, weak'. You could use instruments (such as simple shakers) to enhance. Repeat a few times and then ask a child to be the rhythm maker; swap roles.	Green: *Billy Builds Something Big* Read rhythmic phrases from the book, such as 'He nailed and taped and painted and shaped.' Clap, tap or move to the rhythm of the text. Provide instruments and ask children to create their own rhythms based on selected pieces of text from the story.
Copy or identify pitch/volume	Say some sounds, words or phrases from one of the books using a high or low, loud or quiet, hard or soft voice. Repeat a few times and vary the contrast. Can the children copy your pitch/volume? Can they identify/describe the difference between the way they are said? Then ask a child to be the sound maker; swap roles.	Yellow: *Get to the Airport* Say some phrases from the book using a high/low/loud/quiet/hard/soft voice. For example: • 'We must creep out.' (quiet voice) • 'Not me!' (loud voice) • 'I left my teddy in the car!' (high voice) Ask other groups to describe and copy the others' sounds.
Say it the same way	Ask children to copy a phrase with the same tone, intonation or pattern. Can the children copy the phrase in the same way? Repeat a few times and then ask a child to be the speaker; swap roles.	Blue: *Catch up, Koala!* Say Kangaroo's words using different tones, intonation and pattern: *Catch up, Koala.* Try other phrases, e.g. *Slow down!*
Same or different?	Are these two sounds/rhythms the same or different? Say: *Listen (don't look). Is this sound (clap) the same as this sound (click fingers)?* *Listen. Is this rhythm the same as the next rhythm?* (tap one rhythm and then the same or a different rhythm). Can they say if the sounds/rhythms are the same or different? Repeat a few times and then ask a child to be the speaker or rhythm maker; swap roles.	Blue: *The Magic Paintbox* Clap or click rhythms of sentences from a spread of the book, such as: 'He drew when he woke up.', 'He drew at lunchtime.' See if children can distinguish between them. Ask: *Is this rhythm the same as this rhythm?*
What am I saying?	Say two or three different words or phrases from a book. The words and phrases should each have a different number of syllables and/or different stress pattern. Now say them disguising your voice so children can't hear the words themselves just the rhythm (e.g. whistling or humming). Can the children identify which word or phrase you are saying?	Yellow: *The Quack in the Kitchen* Choose a double page from the book. Read aloud a phrase or sentence, distorting your voice (e.g. in duck quacks). For example, On page 9, contrast: *No, no, no!* with: *Every day, Minu took Socks home.* Can the children identify the phrase/sentence from the double page?

One word or two?	Make some picture cards representing compound words, e.g. on one side of a card show a foot and a generic ball; on the other half of the card show a football. Children listen to the words spoken as either two separate words or as one word, e.g. say, *football* or *foot*, pause, then *ball*. Ask them if they heard one word or two, or to point to the correct picture(s) on the card. Repeat a few times then ask a child to be the speaker; swap roles.	Blue: *Play Outside* Present the words from the text as either one word or two: • foot and steps/footsteps • flower and pot/flowerpot • wood and land/woodland • out and side/outside
Contrastive stress: does it sound right?	Choose some multisyllabic words from a book and say each one with the stress on the correct syllable and with the stress in the wrong place, e.g. PArrot or paRROT. Children listen and repeat the version with the correct stress. Vary the order you present the correct and incorrect stress in each word, so the correct version doesn't always come first.	Green: *Sophie Goes to the Ballet* Say some multisyllabic words from the story and ask which version sounds right, e.g. • danCERS or DANcers • PERformance or perFORMANCE • velVET or VELvet • ORCHestra or orchESTRA
Contrastive intonation: statement or question?	Choose a sentence or phase and say it as a statement or as a question, e.g. Time for lunch! Time for lunch? Children decide from the intonation whether it is a statement or question. Try to avoid examples that use question words (why, which, what, etc.) or structures (Is it…? Are they…? Did…?) as these give clues which are not intonation-related. Repeat a few times and then ask a child to be the speaker; swap roles.	Green: *Toys From 100 Years Ago* Read out some statements from the book as questions (with rising intonation) or as statements: • A spinning top is hollow. • They pulled trucks around a track. • Tricycles are bikes with three wheels. • You can still visit it there today.
Short or dragged out sound?	Ask the children to listen to two ways of saying the same word, e.g. creak or crea-ea-ea-ck. Which is the longest/dragged out sound? Talk about when dragging out might be useful for effect, e.g. The door crea-ea-ea-eaked open. Play a few times and then ask a child to be the speaker; swap roles.	Yellow: *The String* Experiment with some phrases from the story. Which words would work well with dragged out or emphasised pronunciation? • Mooooooooo (page 5) • Oh nooooooo! (page 9) • Hellooooooo! (page 11)

Using *Galaxy books* in guided reading sessions

Rising Stars Reading Planet books are not only designed for independent, individual reading but also as the basis for guided reading sessions. Guided reading is an instructional approach to teaching reading that enables you to devote attention to small groups of children at similar reading ability levels. It allows you to directly teach and support the development of word-reading skills and the skills of reading for meaning.

Organising groups

Ideally, children should be organised into small groups of no more than six. They should have similar reading behaviours and be able to access similar levels of text. Because of the rapidly changing nature of early learners' reading development, you may find that your groups need to remain fluid. The *Galaxy* guided reading lesson plans (see pages 20–67) are presented in a clear, step-by-step format to enable teachers to confidently deliver the sessions with minimal preparation.

Selecting session focuses

Use the book banding/level guidance (page 12), session focus table (page 13), and your own assessment of the group's needs to select a focus for the guided reading session. Be sure to explicitly share this focus with the children and encourage them to reflect and self-assess against the focus at the end of the session. You may wish to have a focus that is based on only word reading or based on only reading for meaning but at these beginner stages it is likely that you will focus on developing the children's ability to read the words and understand the meaning simultaneously.

Structuring the sessions

The lesson plans are based around a three-part guided reading session: Before Reading, During Reading and After Reading.

The Before Reading section gets the children ready to read. In this section, you establish the session focus, introduce the book, revise key phonics knowledge and teach any tricky words that will appear in the book. You can also remind the children of reading strategies such as pointing underneath the graphemes in the word and sounding out slowly to decode the whole word.

In the During Reading section, the children practise their reading skills while you observe and support as required. Over time children will become more independent, but at first you will need to provide plenty of modelling and whole group support. Offer opportunities to pause and reread words and sentences for fluency, and ask questions to check that the children understand what they have read. Remember to offer plenty of praise throughout.

In the After Reading section, the children can reflect on their reading and discuss any challenges they had, such as tricky words or new vocabulary. You can also use the comprehension questions provided to help the children engage with the text and its themes more deeply. This is a good opportunity to relate the story to their own experiences and encourage a love of reading.

Using the independent activities

Each lesson plan is accompanied by a photocopiable worksheet (PCM). These help the children to practise using their reading skills, while also developing their writing, fine motor control, creativity and problem solving. The activities can be used immediately after the guided reading session or at a later time. Ideas are provided to encourage extended engagement with and enjoyment of the text, and can be differentiated according to your children's needs.

Speech rhythm activity

There is a bank of speech rhythm activity ideas on pages 8 and 9. These activities can be used to help develop sensitivity that is an important precursor to learning to read (see page 7 for further information). Try to include one or two of these activities as part of your reading sessions.

Tracking and recording

You can use the group tracking sheets and grids to monitor and record the progress of your children. These are provided on pages 70–71.

Top tips for effective guided reading

Establish routines

Spend time at the beginning of the year establishing routines for guided reading sessions. This could include the time of day that you run the sessions, where children need to sit, where they should collect group resources from. Aim to encourage and increase their independence – this will enable you to concentrate fully on the group you are reading with.

Establish group rules

At the beginning of the year, or even each term, encourage the children to decide on a set of 'rules' or 'courtesies' for the guided reading session. These might include showing others that they are listening by looking at the person speaking, taking turns, trying their best, showing care and respect for books. Establishing rules for the group will help the session run smoothly with minimal interruption.

Be prepared

Think about the resources you might need regularly for guided reading and prepare these in a box that can be quickly accessed. You might include mini-whiteboards and pens, magnetic letters, pre-cut blank cards, a prop such as a hat, highlighters and paper.

Assess and be flexible

Sometimes you will wish to make more formal notes and observations of the children's reading, and sometimes you may wish to informally observe and monitor children's reading. The key to children's progress relies on you being confident to move them fluidly from group to group and adapt the sessions to meet to their reading needs.

Enjoy it!

Guided reading is a wonderful opportunity to spend some focus time with a small group of children really relishing reading as well as developing their skills. Enjoy working with the children, listening to their opinions and watching their reading skills develop.

READING PLANET GALAXY

Using *Galax*y as independent reading scheme books

Children reading *Rising Stars Reading Planet* independently will be able to access the content with minimal adult support. This will enable them to practise and apply the reading skills they have been taught during phonics, guided group reading and general literacy lessons. If you are unsure which level of books a child should read, use an assessment sheet (page 77) to check their word and sentence-reading ability.

Children should be given opportunities to be heard reading one-on-one as often as possible (ideally every day), both at home and in school. This focused attention enables teachers and parents or guardians to monitor and support reading and comprehension on many levels.

You can use independent tracking sheets and grids to monitor and record the progress of each child. These are provided on page 71.

Top tips for effective independent reading

- Provide a comfortable and quiet place to read, with minimal distractions.

- Allow the child to choose what book they want to read from the colour band they are working within.

- Encourage the child to take ownership of the session by asking them to tell you about the book they will be reading.

- Use the inside front and back cover book notes to support the session.

- Remind the reader to decode unknown words from left to right all-through-the-word.

- If readers are stuck, model blending the word for them rather than telling them to guess.

- If the reader requires more blending practice, cover the picture and ask the child to read the sentence and tell you what it means before revealing the picture to check whether they were correct.

- Use the pictures to discuss the story together.

- Encourage the children to reread sentences to gain fluency.

- Model to early readers how to use expression and intonation when reading.

- Use the content of the book to link readers' own experiences.

- Encourage readers to comment upon their opinions of the story.

- Use the reading record as an effective communication tool between school and home.

- Talk naturally about language and text features such as punctuation, informal speech and character names.

*Galax*y book bands/levels

This table shows the different features of the Yellow, Blue, Green and Orange reading books.

Book band/level	Features
Yellow *Reading Planet* Level 3	• may use fantastic/imaginary happenings and environmental text • storylines include several episodes following a time sequence • literary conventions (e.g. Once upon a time) may be used along with familiar oral language structures • characters will be slightly more developed than lower levels • non-fiction texts use personal experience and children's language patterns • illustrations support the text quite closely • may have a variety of print locations on the page • new letter/sound correspondences: ar, or, ur, row, oi, ear, air, ure, er • common exception words: some, one, said, come, do, so, were, when, have, there, out, like, little, what
Blue *Reading Planet* Level 4	• greater variation in sentence patterns and content • literary language is mixed with natural language • stories have more events • development of characters and the prediction of actions and events • non-fiction texts include abstract terms, impersonal sentence structures and sub-headings • contractions may be used and a wider variety of alternate verbs for speech (e.g. called, asked, yelled) • new letter/sound correspondences: wh, ph, ay a-e eigh ey ei a (/long a/), ea e-e ie ey y e (/long e/), ie i-e y i (/long i/), ow o-e oe o (/long o/) • common exception words: some, one, said, come, do, so, were, when, have, there, out, like, little, what
Green *Reading Planet* Level 5	• narrative is non-repetitive and less reliant on familiar experiences • more developed humour, suspense and prediction opportunities in fiction • more varied and larger number of characters, with events sustained over several pages • in non-fiction, texts vocabulary will be less familiar and more specialised • simple captions, headers, fact boxes, contents page, wider range of text types • new letter/sound correspondences: ew ue u-e (/long oo/), ew ue u-e u (/y+oo/), u ou oul (/short oo/), ir er ear or (/er/), ou, oy, eer ere (/ear/), are ear (/air/), our au augh ore (/or/) • common exception words: oh, their, people, Mr, Mrs, looked, called, asked, could, water, where, who, again, thought, through, many, laughed, because, any, eyes, friends, once, please
Orange *Reading Planet* Level 6	• more space allocated on the page to text • more literary language is used and more complex sentence structures, although the meaning of the text is still straightforward • simple non-fiction of different text types are used with texts containing more formal sentences and a wider range of familiar terms • non-fiction texts include section headings, captions, fact boxes, simple charts and diagrams • readers should be able to infer meaning from the text and less literal explanations are needed • new letter/sound correspondences: ch (/k/), ch (/sh/), ce ci cy c esc st se (/s/), ge dge ge gi gy (/j/), le, mb, kn, gn, wr, tch, sion ssion cian tion sure (/sh/ alternatives), ea (/e/), (w) a (/o/), y (/i/) • common exception words: oh, their, people, Mr, Mrs, looked, called, asked, could, water, where, who, again, thought, through, many, laughed, because, any, eyes, friends, once, please

Session focus ideas

Use this table to support you when selecting the session focus for your guided reading groups.

Book band/level	Word reading	Reading for meaning
Yellow *Reading Planet* Level 3	• decoding words ending -ing and -ed • decoding words ending -ing, - er, -est • decoding words ending in -ing and plural 's' • recognising rhyming words • reading high frequency words • recognising common digraphs (e.g. ow, ou) and trigraphs (e.g. ear, air)	• making inferences from the text • drawing on what they already know • being aware of the use of fantastical/imaginary happenings • finding information in non-fiction texts • identifying main events and characters in stories • being aware of more print on the page (including a variety of sentence structures, direct speech, speech bubbles, onomatopoeia, full punctuation)
Blue *Reading Planet* Level 4	• recognising contractions (e.g. don't, you'll) • reading on sight some high frequency words • decoding specialist/unfamiliar words • recognising the use of alternative verbs for 'said' • reading verbs ending in -ing • recognising constituent parts of two-syllable words • decoding two-syllable and three-syllable words	• identifying main events and characters in stories • being aware of more print on the page and variety of print location (some speech bubbles, abstract ideas) • finding information in non-fiction texts • drawing on what they already know • being aware of repetition of phrase patterns and ideas in stories • recognising fantastical elements and story language
Green *Reading Planet* Level 5	• reading words with suffixes -s, -es, -ed, -ing • recognising rhyming endings • using long vowel sounds for decoding • reading common exception words • reading varied and longer sentences • reading two-syllable and three-syllable words • reading less familiar and more complex sentences • reading varied sentences with full punctuation • reading captions, headers, instructions	• exploring poetry with rhythm, rhyme and alliteration • finding information from non-fiction texts • drawing on what they already know • reading aloud using a different voice for different characters • recognising more complex language and full punctuation • reading about people in the past and historical events • distinguishing between fiction and non-fiction texts • identifying characters and events sustained over several pages • repeating words and phrases to check reading accuracy
Orange *Reading Planet* Level 6	• reading on sight high frequency words • reading sentences with full punctuation and speech • decoding polysyllabic words • reading headings, captions and fact boxes • reading two-syllable and three-syllable words • reading less familiar and more complex sentences • reading varied and longer sentences	• identifying characters and events sustained over several pages • exploring the effects of language and phrases • reading non-fiction books for information • reading less familiar and more specialised vocabulary • exploring the effects of fantastical and abstract ideas • reading for information about how people lived in the past • distinguishing between fiction and non-fiction texts

Engaging parents with children's reading

When parents read regularly with their children at home, the benefits are immense. Children make greater reading progress, they are more confident readers and, in many cases, develop a lifelong love of reading. To know how to help parents engage with their children's reading, it's useful to understand the reasons why some parents aren't reading with their children:

- Lack of time – many parents work long hours, or have particularly busy family lives, with other demands on their time.
- Lack of confidence – parents may not be confident readers themselves, or may not speak the English language well.
- Lack of knowledge – parents may not know how to engage and support their children with reading.

There are lots of different ways you can help parents to engage with children's reading. The key to success is to build a whole-school, sustainable, long-term strategy that offers a variety of solutions. The following ideas can be used to reflect on your current provision and contribute to your future planning.

Develop trusting relationships with parents

Even before children start nursery or reception, families are likely to visit your school to get to know the setting and the teachers. This is a key time to start building up trust with parents and ensuring they feel supported. Share the curriculum and emphasise the importance of reading for pleasure. Developing trust with parents at this early stage will make it easier to have meaningful conversations about their child's reading throughout their time at school.

Support EAL parents

If some of the parents speak English as an additional language, consider investing in dual language texts of famous or traditional tales (stories that parents are likely to have encountered before) to help promote discussion about reading at home.

Reading Information Evening

Plan an annual or termly Reading Information Evening. Emphasise to parents both why reading is important and how important it is. Use an infographic, diagram or chart in your presentation to demonstrate visually that the child who doesn't read at home might get around 120 minutes per week of reading practice at school (depending on age and school routines) compared with the child who reads at home and therefore gets that 120 minutes at school plus an additional 210 minutes at home (30 minutes a day). Ask parents to think about that additional 210 minutes per week multiplied over a year – roughly **76,000 minutes more** reading practice for children who read regularly at home.

Parent workshops and drop-in clinics

Host regular, informal reading or phonics workshops and clinics that parents can easily attend. Try holding them at a variety of different times to account for parents' differing working hours. Try to make these sessions as friendly and welcoming as you can – be sure to provide coffee and biscuits. Build positive relationships with parents who attend to help you identify and support their individual concerns and challenges. Listen to their needs and be ready to respond by providing them with information, modelling and resources, or by signposting them to organisations that may help them further, such as local library services or local English language courses.

Open classroom sessions

Invite parents to come into the classroom to join in with reading activities or challenges. This could just be for a regular 'Let's read together' session or might be part of a bigger event. Provide information about how they can engage with their children during the session – you might put activity cards or question cards in the middle of tables or provide details in a letter or on a poster before the session.

Information on the school website

- Reuse content from your Reading Information Evening by uploading a presentation or notes.
- Publish a list of the year's reading events in advance.
- Provide links to other great sources of reading information.
- Upload regular success stories and photographs of reading activities from classrooms.

Highlight reading in your school newsletter

Set aside a dedicated reading section in your school newsletter. Share the stories and nursery rhymes that children are reading or learning in class. Give ideas for activities (such as key word and phonics games) for parents to try at home to kick start conversations around reading.

Provide handouts/leaflets

Keep a stock of handouts or leaflets in the school entrance, or in each classroom, that can be readily given to parents to support them with reading with their child. You might create a sheet providing book-related activity ideas or provide a parent guide like the *Reading Planet Guide to Reading with your Child* (available in multiple languages). This handy guide explains phonic and book banding, and includes tips on how to develop comprehension skills and what to write in a reading record.

Send home book-related activities

Include book-related activities that can be completed at home with parents. Use the photocopy masters (PCMs) in this Teacher Guide to send home inside book bags with the accompanying book. Also, remind parents that the inside front and back covers of the reading books include bite-sized activities that can be enjoyed together.

Plan ahead

Each summer, plan your new school year's reading events. Book dates for book fairs, new author releases, author visits, book-related dress-up days, World Book Day, Reading Information Evenings, parent workshops, drop-in clinics, local library visits and reading challenges. As part of this planning session, be sure to review your current reading resource provision – do you need more reading books? At what levels? In which classrooms?

Consistently promote reading events and successes

It's great to provide a lot of support to parents but you need to keep them engaged by consistently enthusing over reading. Remember to promote reading regularly on the school website, in your newsletters and at assemblies. If you are successful in engaging children with reading at school – they are excited, motivated and receive acknowledgement such as verbal praise or certificates – this enthusiasm will spread into their homes and they will be more likely to help get their parents on board too.

Many thanks to Whittingham Primary Academy for their help in developing this guidance.

How does *Reading Planet* help you to meet National Curriculum requirements?

Year 1

National Curriculum targets	How *Reading Planet* helps to meet these targets
Word reading	
Build on work from the Early Years Foundation Stage, making sure that children can sound out and blend unfamiliar printed words quickly and accurately using the phonics knowledge and skills they have already learnt.	• *Reading Planet* is aligned with this steady progression in teaching and learning, and provides continuous opportunities to revise, practise, apply and consolidate this knowledge so that children learn to read aloud accurately with increasing fluency.
Continue to learn new grapheme-phoneme correspondences (GPCs) and revise and consolidate those learnt earlier. This includes common words containing unusual GPCs (called 'common exception words' or 'tricky words').	• *Reading Planet* supports this by providing reading practice consistent with children's developing phonic knowledge and skill, and their knowledge of common exception words.
Recognise familiar words and work out unfamiliar words by continuing to develop the skill of blending the sounds into words (decoding), and establishing the habit of applying this skill whenever they encounter new words.	• *Reading Planet* books build in new tricky words appropriate to book band levels to broaden children's vocabulary. These are listed on the inside front covers of the books for support and practice before reading.
Read words of more than one syllable, including words containing -s, -es, -ing, -ed, -er and -est endings, and words containing contractions, such as I'm, I'll, we'll.	• *Reading Planet* gradually introduces words of more than one syllable from Pink band onwards. Words with -s and -es ending are introduced from Red band onwards. Words containing -ing, -ed, -er and -est endings are included from Yellow band. Contractions are introduced from Blue band.
Reading comprehension	
Develop reading for pleasure and expanding vocabulary by listening to and reading aloud a wide range of stories (including fairy stories and traditional tales), poems and non-fiction.	• *Reading Planet* has been developed with reading for pleasure in mind, and includes engaging and enjoyable fiction and non-fiction titles. It contains retellings of traditional tales and fairy stories, rhyming stories and poetry collections, particularly within the *Galaxy* strand.
Demonstrating understanding when talking about what they have read or have listened to, and linking this to their own experiences. Discussing the title, making inferences, predicting what will happen next and explaining understanding of a text.	• Comprehension questions are included on the back page of the reading books to allow an adult to check understanding and relate the content to the child's personal experience and/or knowledge.

READING PLANET GALAXY

Year 2 (deepens and builds on the Year 1 requirements – below are the notable additional aims for Year 2)

National Curriculum targets	How *Reading Planet* meets these requirements
Word reading	
Children should be able to read all common graphemes, and read unfamiliar words containing these graphemes accurately and fluently without overt blending.	• *Reading Planet* supports this by providing books that are consistent with children's developing phonic knowledge and skill. All GPCs are covered across the scheme. The Assessment support materials within this guide can help to track progress and reading accuracy.
Read a wider range of common exception words and containing common suffixes, such as -ly, -ful, -ness.	• *Reading Planet* lists common exception words on the inside front cover of each book. The books build in an increasing range of suffixes from Blue and Green bands onwards.
Reading comprehension	
Explain, discuss and express views about an increasing range of books, including poetry, stories and non-fiction.	• *Reading Planet* provides a wide range of genres and non-fiction across the scheme. The lesson plans designed for guided group reading include questions to ask and activities to use after reading to support understanding and discussion.
Retrieve and explain relevant details from fiction and non-fiction to demonstrate understanding of character, events and information.	• The comprehension questions at the end of each book, and the guided group reading lesson plans, provide opportunities for discussion of these specific aspects.
Identify and discuss the sequence of events in texts and how these are related.	• At the end of each fiction title, children are encouraged to retell the story in their own words, which reinforces understanding of the sequence of events. Some activity sheets in the guided group reading lesson plans also involve sequencing.
Read non-fiction books that are structured in different ways.	• *Reading Planet* contains a range of non-fiction books including, biographies, recounts, information books and picture atlases that present factual information in a range of ways.

Reading Planet and the National Tests (SATs)

Reading Planet books have been carefully designed to provide children with practice in using the full range of cognitive processes required to meet the expected standards in the national tests. This means that the texts have been written to stimulate and encourage the thinking skills required to respond effectively to test-style questions. The questions at the back of the books and the guided reading lesson plans also prepare children for the areas they will be questioned on at the end of Key Stage 1, notably:

- drawing on knowledge of vocabulary to understand texts
- identifying and explaining key aspects of fiction and non-fiction texts, such as characters, events, titles and information
- identifying the sequence of events in texts
- making inferences
- predicting what might happen on the basis of what has been read so far.

See pages 68–69 for further guidance.

International Phonetic Alphabet chart

This chart shows the focus graphemes used within the Yellow, Blue, Green and Orange levels of *Galaxy*. The chart is useful as a pronunciation guide and includes the International Phonetic Alphabet (IPA) as well as prompt words to support 'saying the sounds'.

IPA	Grapheme/s	Prompt word	Book band
/ɑː/	ar	car	Yellow
/ɔː/	or	fork	Yellow
/ɜː/	ur	curl	Yellow
/aʊ/	ow	cow	Yellow
/ɔɪ/	oi	oil	Yellow
/ɪə/	ear	near	Yellow
/ɛə/	air	hair	Yellow
/j/+/ʊə/	ure	cure	Yellow
/ɜː/	er	person	Yellow
/w/	wh	white	Blue
/f/	ph	elephant	Blue
/eɪ/	ay; a-e; eigh; ey; ei; a	cake	Blue
/iː/	ea; e-e; ie; y; e	sea	Blue
/aɪ/	ie; i-e; y; i	tie	Blue
/əʊ/	ow; o-e; oe; o	boat	Blue
/uː/	ew; ue; u-e	June	Green
/juː/	ew; ue; u-e; u	rescue	Green
/ʊ/	u; ou; oul	could	Green
/ɜː/	ir; er; ear; or	bird	Green
/aʊ/	ou	shout	Green
/ɔɪ/	oy	toy	Green
/ear/	eer; ere	deer	Green
/ɛə/	are; ear	bear	Green
/ɔː/	our; au; augh; ore; al; oar; oor	four	Green
/k/	ch	school	Orange
/ʃ/	ch	chef	Orange
/s/	ce; ci; cy; ce; sc; st; se	circle	Orange
/dʒ/	ge; dge; ge; gi; gy	giant	Orange
/əl/	le	bottle	Orange
/m/	mb	comb	Orange
/n/	kn; gn	gnome	Orange
/r/	wr	write	Orange
/tʃ/	tch	fetch	Orange
/ʃən/	sion; ssion; cian; tion	optician	Orange
/ʒə/	sure	treasure	Orange
/ɛ/	ea	bread	Orange
/ɒ/	(w)a	watch	Orange
/ɪ/	y	cymbals	Orange
/ʒ/	si	television	Orange

Phonics progression mapping/alignment

Book title	Book band/level	Letters and Sounds phase	New phoneme-grapheme correspondences	New common exception words
The Quack in the Kitchen	Yellow Level 3	Phase 3/4	ar, or, ur, ow, oi, ear, air, ure, er	some, one, said, come, do, so, were, when, have, there, out, like, little, what
Be a Good Friend				
Get to the Airport				
Teddy Bears				
The String				
Picture a Sunset				
The Magic Paintbox	Blue Level 4	Phase 4/5	wh ph ay a-e eigh ey ei a /long a/ ea e-e ie ey y e /long e/ ie i-e y i /long i/ ow o-e oe o /long o/	some, one, said, come, do, so, were, when, have, there, out, like, little, what
Into the Woods				
Catch Up, Koala!				
Amazing Animation				
Vanya the Viking				
Play Outside				
Rumpelstiltskin	Green Level 5	Phase 5	ew ue u-e /long oo/ ew ue u-e u /y+oo/ u ou oul /short oo/ ir er ear or /er/ ou oy eer ere /ear/ are ear /air/ our au augh ore /or/	oh, their, people, Mr, Mrs, looked, called, asked, could, water, where, who, again, thought, through, many, laughed, because, any, eyes, friends, once, please
Toys From 100 Years Ago				
Sophie Goes to the Ballet				
My Super Senses				
Billy Builds Something Big				
My Nature Activity Book				
Robin Hood and the Golden Arrow	Orange Level 6	Phase 5/6	ch /k/ ch /sh/ ce ci cy ce sc st se /s/ g edge ge gi gy /j/ le mb kn gn wr tch sion ssion cian tion sure /sh/ alternatives ea /e/ (w)a /o/	oh, their, people, Mr, Mrs, looked, called, asked, could, water, where, who, again, thought, through, many, laughed, because, any, eyes, friends, once, please
Incredible Creatures from Greek Myths				
The Samurai's Brave Daughter				
Richard and the Lions				
The Jumpy Bumpy Feeling				
Laugh Out Loud				

THE QUACK IN THE KITCHEN

Yellow

GUIDED GROUP READING

BEFORE READING

Book introduction:
- Look together at the cover image, title and blurb of the book. Ask: *What do you think the 'quack' in the kitchen could be? What type of book is this?* (fiction, humour)
- Point to the speech bubbles and sound effects. Tell the children to read these after the main text on each page.
- Use flashcards or mini whiteboards to revise the following Yellow letter/sound correspondences: **ar, or, ur, ow, ear, er**.
- Share and practise reading or sounding out the tricky words in this book: **Minu, saw, bird, eat, worm, fluffy, their, every, day, say, away, miaow, wants, home, heard, taken, water, bowl, warm, loves, watching**.
- Discuss the meaning of any unfamiliar words or phrases.

Strategy check:
- Encourage the children to use phonics skills to decode any new words. If they struggle, remind them to use a range of reading strategies, e.g. saying and blending letter sounds, reading root words before endings, deciding if the text makes sense, seeing a known word or sound within a word, using picture cues and developing basic inference and deduction skills.
- Ask questions to encourage these skills, e.g. *What can you do when you come to a word that you don't know?*

DURING READING

Independent reading:
- Encourage the children to read independently while you listen to each child in the group in turn.
- If a child struggles to read 90% of the text independently, review their current reading band.
- Model sounding out and blending, or ask individuals to decode words to the group.
- Highlight examples of successful problem-solving. Say: *You saw that 'duckling' and 'jingling' ended with the same sound. Well done!*
- If appropriate, pause occasionally to reread a sentence, check for understanding and discuss the illustrations. Ask: *How can we tell it is spring from the picture (on pages 2–3)?*
Do you think Socks is a good name for Minu's cat (on pages 6–7)? Why/why not?
Why did Minu say "No, no, no!" on page 9?
Why did Socks need a bell (on page 13)?

AFTER READING

Return to the text:
- Share any words that caused difficulty with decoding, pronunciation or understanding.
- Challenge the children to create phrases/sentences using the tricky words *saw, worm, warm, bird*.
- Encourage the children to reflect on their learning. Ask: *Do you think Socks will visit the ducklings again? Was the bell on his collar a good idea? Can you explain why?*
- Use the comprehension questions at the end of the book to talk about the story and animals that live indoors and outdoors.
- Ask some of the following additional questions to check understanding of the text and explore the themes:
Do you think Minu is a caring person? How do you know?
Did you like the story ending? Explain why.
What would you have done to stop Socks from taking the ducklings?

Follow-up activities:
1. Use the PCM provided to review the children's understanding of the story. The children write the correct words in the gaps to complete the sentences.
2. Ask the children: *Why do cats chase birds?* Find out what other animals eat, using information books and/or appropriate children's websites. The children can then choose an animal (such as a dog, horse, lion, snake, bird, etc.) and draw and label pictures of it with its food.

BOOK OVERVIEW

Minu likes to visit the pond at a nearby park to look at the newly hatched ducklings, but one day she notices that her cat, Socks, has followed them and is interested in the ducklings too! After Socks brings one of the ducklings home, Dad cleverly suggests that Socks should wear a bell on his collar, so that the ducklings know he is coming!

The Quack in the Kitchen

Name: _____ Date: _____

Write the correct words in the gaps to complete the sentences.

1. It was _____ and Minu was at the park.

spring   summer   autumn   winter

2. Then Minu saw _____ fluffy ducklings!

two   ten   twenty

3. Dad said, "Socks wants to _____."

catch a fish   catch a duckling   catch a rat

4. A duckling was swimming in _____!

the cat's water bowl   the swimming pool   the bath

5. Dad said, "Socks needs a _____ …"

bowl   collar   bell

Reading Planet Galaxy © Rising Stars UK Ltd 2018. You may photocopy this page.

BE A GOOD FRIEND

Yellow

GUIDED GROUP READING

BEFORE READING

Book introduction:
- Look together at the cover image, title and blurb of the book. Ask: *What is a 'good friend'? What does a good friend do?*
- Talk about 'feelings' and how our friends can help us to feel better.
- Use flashcards or mini whiteboards to revise the following Yellow letter/sound correspondences: **or, ur, ow, er**.
- Share and practise reading or sounding out the tricky words in this book: **happy, friend, give, your, shy, lonely, play, ball, take, worried, comfort, gone, may, our, own, share**.
- Discuss the meaning of any unfamiliar words or phrases, such as: **come and go, comfort**.

Strategy check:
- Encourage the children to use phonics skills to decode any new words. If they struggle, remind them to use a range of reading strategies, e.g. saying and blending letter sounds, reading root words before endings, deciding if the text makes sense, seeing a known word or sound within a word, using picture cues and developing basic inference and deduction skills.
- Ask questions to encourage these skills, e.g. *What can you do when you come to a word that you don't know?*

DURING READING

Independent reading:
- Encourage the children to read independently while you listen to each child in the group in turn.
- If a child struggles to read 90% of the text independently, review their current reading band.
- Model sounding out and blending, or ask individuals to decode words to the group.
- Highlight examples of successful problem-solving. Say: *Recognising the word 'feel' helped you to decode the word 'feelings'. Well done!*
- If appropriate, pause occasionally to reread a sentence, check for understanding and discuss the illustrations. Ask: *Why do you think Adam is frowning on page 8? Why is Asha happier in the second picture on page 9? What is Ruby worried about on page 10? What is Devam doing in the second picture on page 11? Does it help to be on our own when we are cross (on pages 12–13)? Why/why not?*

AFTER READING

Return to the text:
- Share any words that caused difficulty with decoding, pronunciation or understanding.
- Show the children how to divide the words *un/til, frown/ing* and *feel/ings* into two syllables to help with decoding.
- Encourage the children to reflect on their learning. Ask: *How do we show our feelings to others? Why is it good to share our feelings?*
- Use the comprehension questions at the end of the book to talk about the story and how to be a good friend.
- Ask some of the following additional questions to check understanding of the story and explore the themes: *Is it better to leave someone alone when they feel sad? Why/why not? What could you say to someone who feels lonely? Is it good to tell someone when we need help? Why?*

Follow-up activities:
1. Using the PCM provided, the children recall details from the book and match words to pictures. They revise vocabulary from the book and practise writing words accurately.
2. Cut out pictures of faces from old magazines. Ask the children to think of words that describe the emotions shown by each face. Create a 'feelings vocabulary' with new words, e.g. excited, embarrassed, proud, frustrated, thrilled, joyful. Ask the children to make up short conversations between imaginary characters using the faces.
3. Ask the children to complete sentences about their feelings, e.g. *I feel happy when…, I feel excited when…, I feel proud when….*

BOOK OVERVIEW

Sometimes we can feel sad, angry or lonely. In this non-fiction book, the children learn how they can address these different emotions, and how to be there when a friend needs help, comfort or reassurance.

Be a Good Friend

Name: _____ Date: _____

Write one word to complete each of the sentences below. Choose from the words in the box. You can use the book to help you.

Chen is _____.   Ella feels _____.

Ranjit looks _____.   Adam is _____.

Ruby is _____.   Devam is _____.

| afraid   frowning   shy   sad   worried   lonely |

GET TO THE AIRPORT

Yellow

GUIDED GROUP READING

BEFORE READING

Book introduction:

- Look together at the cover image, title and blurb of the book. Ask: *Who has been to an airport? Why did you go there?*
- Discuss what 'passports' are and what 'checking in' means.
- Use flashcards or mini whiteboards to revise the following Yellow letter/sound correspondences: **ar, or, ur, oi, air, er**.
- Share and practise reading or sounding out the tricky words in this book: **holiday, time, everyone, smallest, teddy, airport, pulled, their, silly, your, Daddy**.
- Discuss the meaning of any unfamiliar words or phrases, such as: **went bright red**.

Strategy check:

- Encourage the children to use phonics skills to decode any new words. If they struggle, remind them to use a range of reading strategies, e.g. saying and blending letter sounds, reading root words before endings, deciding if the text makes sense, seeing a known word or sound within a word, using picture cues and developing basic inference and deduction skills.
- Ask questions to encourage these skills, e.g. *What can you do when you come to a word that you don't know?*

DURING READING

Independent reading:

- Encourage the children to read independently while you listen to each child in the group in turn.
- Model sounding out and blending, or ask individuals to decode words to the group.
- Highlight examples of successful problem-solving. Say: *You split the word 'passport' into two words to help you read it. Well done!*
- Encourage the children to recognise repeated words: *Shhh! Silly Lena! Silly Daddy!*
- If appropriate, pause occasionally to reread a sentence, check for understanding and discuss the illustrations. Ask: *What time was it when they had to get up (on page 3)?*
What did Lena mean when she said, "Not me!" on page 5?
Why do they need passports (on page 7)?
Why did Dad go 'bright red' on page 13?
Why did Lena say, "Silly Daddy!" on page 15?

AFTER READING

Return to the text:

- Share any words that caused difficulty with decoding, pronunciation or understanding. Divide the words *air/port* and *pass/port* into two beats or parts.
- Highlight the root words in the past tense verbs: *dressed, yelled, picked, started, turned, pulled, checked, pointed*.
- Encourage the children to reflect on their learning. Ask: *What would have happened if Dad had forgotten their passports? How do you think Dad felt at the end of the story?*
- Use the comprehension questions at the end of the book to talk about the story and the children's experiences of going on holiday.
- Ask some of the following additional questions to check understanding of the story and explore the themes:
Lena took her teddy – what do you take on holiday with you?
Who was the most excited about going on holiday? Explain why.
Why do we have passports?
Where can we go on holiday without a passport?

Follow-up activities:

1. Using the PCM provided, the children practise using appropriate punctuation by writing an exclamation mark or question mark at the end of each sentence. This also provides an opportunity to revise key vocabulary from the story.
2. Support the children to make their own passports. Ask them to draw a picture of themselves and write their full name and details below, e.g. their birthday. They can make passports for other family members too.
3. Make a list of compound words, starting with examples found in the text: *airport, passport, everyone*. Think of others, inspired by the book's theme: *suitcase, runway, seatbelt*.

BOOK OVERVIEW

Maxim and Lena are going on holiday with Mum and Dad. They have to get up and out in the dark of the night, but Lena finds it very hard to be quiet! After nearly leaving without Lena's teddy, they get into the terminal to find Dad may not have the passports after all!

Get to the Airport

Name: _____ Date: _____

Add an exclamation mark or question mark to complete each sentence. You can use the book to help you.

"Not me ___" yelled Lena.

Have you got the passports ___

"Are we there yet ___" yelled Lena.

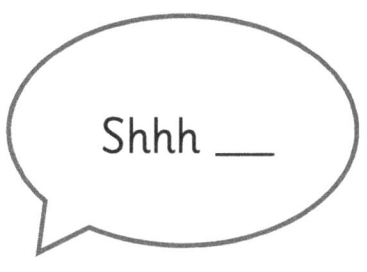

Shhh ___

"Silly Lena ___" said Dad.

Can I see your passports ___

"There they are ___" yelled Lena.

TEDDY BEARS

Yellow

GUIDED GROUP READING

BEFORE READING

Book introduction:

- Look together at the cover image, title and blurb of the book. Ask: *Who has got a teddy bear? Does your teddy have a name?*
- Discuss the reasons why children (and adults) like teddies.
- Use flashcards or mini whiteboards to revise the following Yellow letter/sound correspondences: **or**, **er**.
- Share and practise reading or sounding out the tricky words in this book: **Teddy, very, bear, ago, new, name, want, toy, your, made, gave, about, Winne the Pooh, Rupert, Story, today, give, their, take, which**.
- Discuss the meaning of any unfamiliar words or phrases, such as: **fabric**.

Strategy check:

- Encourage the children to use phonics skills to decode any new words. If they struggle, remind them to use a range of reading strategies, e.g. saying and blending letter sounds, reading root words before endings, deciding if the text makes sense, seeing a known word or sound within a word, using picture cues and developing basic inference and deduction skills.
- Ask questions to encourage these skills, e.g. *What can you do when you come to a word that you don't know?*

DURING READING

Independent reading:

- Encourage the children to read independently while you listen to each child in the group in turn.
- If the children struggle to read independently, review their current reading band.
- Model sounding out and blending, or ask individuals to decode words to the group.
- Highlight examples of successful problem-solving. Say: *You knew the word 'old' so you could work out the word 'sold'. Well done!*
- If appropriate, pause occasionally to reread a sentence, check for understanding and discuss the illustrations. Ask: *How do you know this teddy is old on page 2? Who is called Teddy on page 4? Have you ever been to a teddy bears' picnic (on page 13)? Which is your favourite teddy (on pages 14–15)?*

AFTER READING

Return to the text:

- Share any words that caused difficulty with decoding, pronunciation or understanding. Demonstrate how to split the word 'important' into three parts: *im/por/tant*.
- Encourage the children to reflect on their learning. Ask: *Which of the teddies in the book was the oldest? How do you know?*
- Use the comprehension questions at the end of the book to talk about teddy bears and children's stories that feature them.
- Ask some of the following additional questions to check understanding of the text and explore the themes:
Do you think your parents had teddy bears when they were children?
What is the difference between a toy teddy and a real bear?
Why do you think toy bears are more popular than, say, toy rabbits or toy giraffes?

Follow-up activities:

1. Using the PCM provided, the children revise vocabulary from the book, and practise writing words accurately by imagining what two teddies might say to each other when they meet. They write a few words in the speech bubbles, supported by words from the book.
2. Invite the children to bring their teddy bears in to the classroom. Sitting in a circle with the teddies, ask the children to take turns to read teddy bear-themed stories and poems to the teddies.
3. List words that rhyme with 'bear'. Highlight words that sound the same but are spelt differently, e.g. hare/hair, fare/fair, pear/pair, wear/ware, stare/stair.

BOOK OVERVIEW

Teddy bears are very old toys, but where do they come from? This book takes a look at the history of teddy bears, their origins and how they have become an important childhood toy for generations.

Teddy Bears

Name: _____   Date: _____

What are the teddies saying? Write on the lines.
You can use words from the box below to help you.

Hello.

My name is _____.

I am _____.

Hello.

My name is _____.

I am _____.

| soft | new | old | sad | bear |

Reading Planet Galaxy © Rising Stars UK Ltd 2018. You may photocopy this page.

THE STRING

Yellow

GUIDED GROUP READING

BEFORE READING

Book introduction:
- Look together at the cover image, title and blurb of the book. Ask: *What type of book do you think this is?* (fiction, traditional tale)
- Point to the sound effects (e.g. *Chop! Moo! Cluck! Splash!*). Tell the children to think about the way these sound in real life when they read them.
- Use flashcards or mini whiteboards to revise the following Yellow letter/sound correspondences: **or, ar, ow, er**.
- Share and practise reading or sounding out the tricky words in this book: **over, round, birds, used, way, sea, oh, beach, giant, hole, hello, found, new, friends**.
- Discuss the meaning of any unfamiliar words or phrases, such as: **chicken coop, steep**.

Strategy check:
- Encourage the children to use phonics skills to decode any new words. If they struggle, remind them to use a range of reading strategies, e.g. saying and blending letter sounds, reading root words before endings, deciding if the text makes sense, seeing a known word or sound within a word, using picture cues and developing basic inference and deduction skills.
- Ask questions to encourage these skills, e.g. *What can you do when you come to a word that you don't know?*

DURING READING

Independent reading:
- Encourage the children to read independently while you listen to each child in the group in turn.
- Model sounding out and blending, or ask individuals to decode words to the group.
- Highlight examples of successful problem-solving. Say: *You were able to work out the word 'fisherman' by breaking it into syllables: fish/er/man. Well done!*
- Tell the children to read the sound effects with expression: *Moo! Cluck! Splash!*
- If appropriate, pause occasionally to reread a sentence, check for understanding and discuss the illustrations. Ask: *When do you think this story took place (on pages 2–3)?*
Where did the string lead to first? (page 4)
How are the birds using the string (on page 8)?
Why did Patrick say, "Oh no!" on page 9?
Does the giant look friendly (on page 11)? Explain why.

AFTER READING

Return to the text:
- Share any words that caused difficulty with decoding, pronunciation or understanding.
- Encourage the children to reflect on their learning. Ask: *Why did the giant say, "And I found some new friends!"? Do you think Patrick and his grandad will see the giant again? Say why.*
- Use the comprehension questions at the end of the book to talk about giants and children's stories that feature them.
- Ask some of the following additional questions to check understanding of the text and explore the themes:
Did Patrick and his grandad know that the string came from a giant at the start of the story?
Do you think this story is true? Explain why.
What would be a good name for the giant in this story?
Will Patrick and his grandad have other adventures with the giant?

Follow-up activities:
1. Using the PCM provided, the children revise key vocabulary from the story by reading the words in the signposts and colouring these in.
2. Make a list of words to describe the giant in the story. As a class, compose descriptive sentences, e.g. 'He was as tall as the tallest tree in the forest. His feet were like huge logs and his hands were like waving branches.'
3. Act out the events in the story using puppets or role-play. Can the children remember the correct order of events? Check by rereading the book.

BOOK OVERVIEW

Patrick and his grandad are confused when they discover the end of a piece of string outside their house. They follow the string through a farmyard, a wood and across the sea, finally arriving at the bottom of a steep cliff. At the top, they discover the end is attached to the jumper of a very friendly giant, who offers to take them on the long journey back home.

The String

Name: _____ **Date:** _____

Follow the string with your pencil. Read the words along the way. When you can read a word, colour it in.

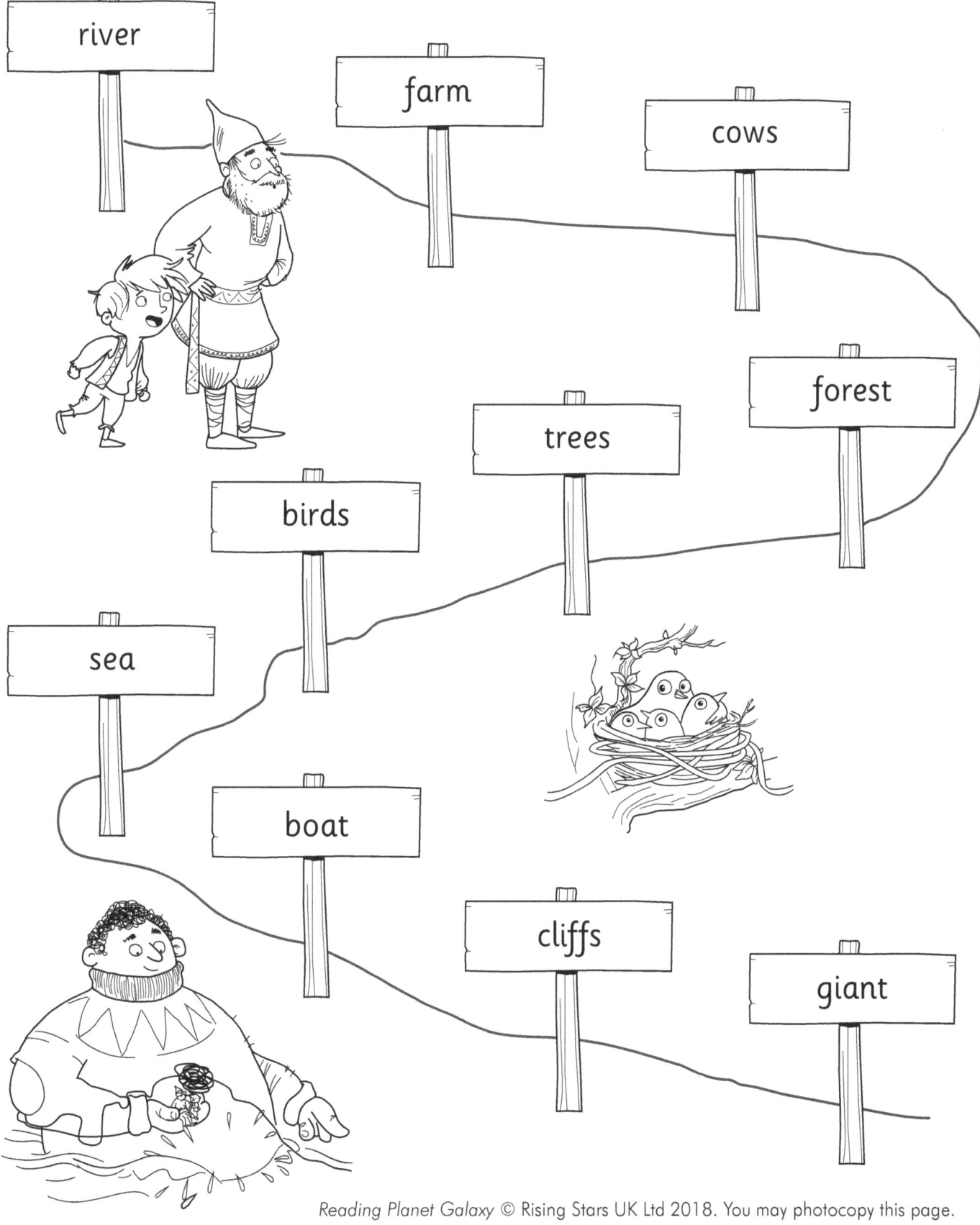

PICTURE A SUNSET

Yellow

GUIDED GROUP READING

BEFORE READING

Book introduction:
- Look together at the cover image, title and blurb of the book. Ask: *What is a sunset? Who has seen one?*
- Discuss the difference between 'sunrise' and 'sunset'.
- Use flashcards or mini whiteboards to revise the following Yellow letter/sound correspondences: **ar**, **ur**, **ure**, **er**.
- Share and practise reading or sounding out the tricky words in this book: **know**, **day**, **sunrise**, **sky**, **colours**, **make**, **picture**, **photograph**, **clouds**, **yellow**, **gold**, **blue**, **orange**, **your**, **paper**, **pencil**, **draw**, **wash**, **glue**, **dry**, **use**, **show**.
- Discuss the meaning of any unfamiliar words or phrases, such as: **dab**.

Strategy check:
- Encourage the children to use phonics skills to decode any new words. If they struggle, remind them to use a range of reading strategies, e.g. saying and blending letter sounds, reading root words before endings, deciding if the text makes sense, seeing a known word or sound within a word, using picture cues and developing basic inference and deduction skills.
- Ask questions to encourage these skills, e.g. *What can you do when you come to a word that you don't know?*

DURING READING

Independent reading:
- Encourage the children to read independently while you listen to each child in the group in turn.
- Remind the children to track underneath the words with their finger and to read all the words, as some text appears in different places on the page.
- Model sounding out and blending, or ask individuals to decode words to the group.
- Highlight examples of successful problem-solving. Say: *You split the word 'fantastic' into three parts then blended them correctly. Well done!*
- If appropriate, pause occasionally to reread a sentence, check for understanding and discuss the illustrations. Ask: *Why are there arrows in the illustration on pages 2–3?*
What would you add to your sunset picture (on page 9)?
Why are there numbers in the text on pages 10–11?
Do you think you might see a sunset tonight (page 15)?

AFTER READING

Return to the text:
- Share any words that caused difficulty with decoding, pronunciation or understanding. Point out the /ph/ sounds in the word *photograph*.
- Encourage the children to reflect on their learning. Ask: *Can we see sunsets every night? If not, why not?*
- Use the comprehension questions at the end of the book to talk about sunsets and how we can make sunset pictures.
- Ask some of the following additional questions to check understanding of the text and explore the themes:
Return to the book's title 'Picture a Sunset' – what does this mean?
Has anyone ever made a sunset picture before?
Are there any other ways of making a sunset picture? What would you do differently?

Follow-up activities:
1. Using the PCM provided, the children practise their reading skills by creating their own sunset picture and then adding appropriate text labels to it.
2. The children can make their own sunset pictures by following the instructions in the book.
3. Challenge the children to think of as many different names for colours as they can. Ask the children to choose their favourite colour names from paint brochures and explain their choices, e.g. 'That colour makes me think of …'.

BOOK OVERVIEW

What is a sunset and how can we show it as a picture? Find out in this non-fiction book which provides both science explanations and some simple, step-by-step instructions for how to create a sunset picture.

Picture a Sunset

Name: _____   Date: _____

Draw your own sunset. Use lots of colours. Cut out the labels and stick them to your picture.

sunset	land	Sun
clouds	sky	yellow
gold	lilac	blue
	orange	pink

Reading Planet Galaxy © Rising Stars UK Ltd 2018. You may photocopy this page.

THE MAGIC PAINTBOX
Blue

GUIDED GROUP READING

BEFORE READING

Book introduction:
- Look together at the cover image, title and blurb of the book. Ask: *What does the word 'magic' mean? How could a paintbox be magic?*
- Use flashcards or mini whiteboards to revise the following Blue letter/sound correspondences: **wh, ay a-e a (long a), ea y e (long e), i-e (long i), ow o-e o (long o)**.
- Share and practise reading or sounding out the tricky words in this book: **drawing, drew, before, parcel, water, dinosaurs, walls, jungle, used, colours, know, magic, taller, first, excited, roar, found, picture, house, door, tomorrow**.
- Discuss the meaning of any unfamiliar words or phrases, such as: **grunt**.

Strategy check:
- Encourage the children to use phonics skills to decode any new words. If they struggle, remind them to use a range of reading strategies, e.g. saying and blending letter sounds, reading root words before endings, deciding if the text makes sense, seeing a known word or sound within a word, using picture cues and developing basic inference and deduction skills.
- Ask questions to encourage these skills, e.g. *What can you do when you come to a word that you don't know?*

DURING READING

Independent reading:
- Encourage the children to read independently while you listen to each child in the group in turn.
- If a child struggles to read 90% of the text independently, review their current reading band.
- Model sounding out and blending, or ask individuals to decode words to the group.
- Highlight examples of successful problem-solving. Say: *You split the word 'to-morr-ow' perfectly to decode it. Well done!*
- If appropriate, pause occasionally to reread a sentence, check for understanding and discuss the illustrations. Ask: *What do you think Art was drawing (on pages 2–3)? How do you know Art was pleased with his box of paints (on pages 4–5)? What was happening to the trees on page 8? Why did Art think he was lost (on page 11)? What do you think will happen next (on page 13)?*

AFTER READING

Return to the text:
- Share any words that caused difficulty with decoding, pronunciation or understanding, e.g. volcano – the first /o/ is short, but the final /o/ is long.
- Challenge the children to think of other words that end in /o/, e.g. potato, tomato.
- Encourage the children to reflect on their learning. Ask: *How did Art feel at the start of the story? What about the middle? What about the end?*
- Use the comprehension questions at the end of the book to talk about the story and the things the children like to draw.
- Ask some of the following additional questions to check understanding of the story and explore the themes: *Do you think Art's grandad knew the paints were magic? What do you think happened to the jungle and the dinosaurs at the end? Did you like Art's plan to get home? Say why.*

Follow-up activities:
1. Using the PCM provided, the children recall the main events in the story. They practise their sequencing skills by cutting out the sentences and numbering them in the correct order. They can then use these sentences to retell the story.
2. Challenge the children to rewrite/redraw the story ending by thinking of something else Art could have drawn to escape the dinosaurs, e.g. a big cage in a zoo or a huge hole! Ask: *How would this have changed the story ending?*
3. Tell the children to imagine they have a magic paintbox. Ask them to draw a picture of a place they would like to go to. Using this idea, they can go on to create an alternative book cover for the reader.

BOOK OVERVIEW

Art receives a brand-new box of paints from his grandad in the post. He starts to paint straightaway and quickly discovers that whatever he creates comes to life, including some very large and scary dinosaurs! Thankfully, quick-witted Art comes up with a painting plan to get back home.

The Magic Paintbox

Name: _____ Date: _____

Cut out the sentences. Place them in the correct order and number them. Use them to retell the story in your own words.

Art painted some dinosaurs.

Art was very good at drawing.

The magic picture faded away.

The picture of his house came to life.

All of a sudden, the dinosaurs began to stamp and grunt and roar.

Art found a box of paints inside the parcel.

INTO THE WOODS

Blue

GUIDED GROUP READING

BEFORE READING

Book introduction:
- Look together at the cover image, title and blurb of the book. Ask: *How is Barnaby Bear travelling the world in this book? Have you ever been to the woods – what did you see there?*
- Use flashcards or mini whiteboards to revise the following Blue letter/sound correspondences: **wh, ay ey a (long a), ea e-e y e (long e), i-e y (long i), ow o-e o (long o)**.
- Share and practise reading or sounding out the tricky words in this book: **South, Scotland, today, Bear, beetles, leaves, other, world, two, Jungle, monkey, watches, wants, honey, love, ice, penguins**.
- Discuss the meaning of any unfamiliar words or phrases, such as: **north, west, east, south, lush, vine**.

Strategy check:
- Encourage the children to use phonics skills to decode any new words. If they struggle, remind them to use a range of reading strategies, e.g. saying and blending letter sounds, reading root words before endings, deciding if the text makes sense, seeing a known word or sound within a word, using picture cues and developing basic inference and deduction skills.
- Ask questions to encourage these skills, e.g. *What can you do when you come to a word that you don't know?*

DURING READING

Independent reading:
- Encourage the children to read independently while you listen to each child in the group in turn.
- Model sounding out and blending, or ask individuals to decode words to the group.
- Turn to pages 2–3 and, pointing to the map, ask the children: *What is this?* (a map) *What does the map show us?* Explain the compass points.
- Highlight examples of successful problem-solving. Say: *You read the contraction 'I'll' without much hesitation. Well done!*
- If appropriate, pause occasionally to reread a sentence, check for understanding and discuss the illustrations. Ask: *Why is white a good colour for an Arctic fox (on page 7)? Why did Snowy Owl point to a beehive (on page 12)?*

AFTER READING

Return to the text:
- Share any words that caused difficulty with decoding, pronunciation or understanding.
- Challenge the children to say what the missing sounds are in the contractions: *I'll, that's*. Ask: *What would the words become if we put back the missing letters?*
- Encourage the children to reflect on their learning. Ask: *Can you name all the animals Barnaby met in the woods? Which was your favourite? Say why.*
- Use the comprehension questions at the end of the book to talk about the text and the countries and animals visited.
- Ask some of the following additional questions to check understanding of the book and explore the themes:
Where did Barnaby see the moose?
Which two animals did Barnaby see in the jungle?
Is India in the west or east?
Can you remember the names of the countries that Barnaby Bear visited?
Which of the places that Barnaby visited had snow?

Follow-up activities:
1. Using the PCM provided, the children think creatively about the book by writing about a place they would like to visit, drawing an animal they might meet there, and writing a sentence about what their animal might eat.
2. As a class, list words from the book with the /oo/ sound, i.e. moose, roots, hoots, swoop. Discuss other similar words and add them to your list, e.g. goose, loose, whoosh, hoop, loop, snoop, etc. Ask: *Can you find an /oo/ word in the book that makes a different sound?* (e.g. 'woods')

BOOK OVERVIEW

Barnaby Bear goes on an adventure with Snowy Owl around the woods of the world. By the time he's seen Scotland, Norway, America and India, Barnaby is almost too tired to realise that there are no woods in Antarctica… but there are lots of penguins!

Into the Woods

Name: _____ Date: _____

Where would you like to fly to?

I would fly to _____

because _____

_____.

Draw a picture of an animal that you might meet there.

What do you think your animal likes to eat? Write it in a sentence below.

My animal likes to eat _____.

CATCH UP, KOALA!

Blue

GUIDED GROUP READING

BEFORE READING

Book introduction:
- Look together at the cover image, title and blurb of the book. Ask: *Where do you think this story takes place? Where do koalas and kangaroos come from?*
- Explain that the 'big red rock' on the cover is Uluru, a famous landmark in Australia.
- Use flashcards or mini whiteboards to revise the following Blue letter/sound correspondences: **ay a-e ey a (long a), y e (long e), i-e y (long i), ow o-e o (long o)**.
- Share and practise reading or sounding out the tricky words in this book: **ago, koala, friends, only, already, shouted, Emu's, ball, any, would, falling, edge, two, watched**.
- Discuss the meaning of any unfamiliar words or phrases, such as: **set off**.

Strategy check:
- Encourage the children to use phonics skills to decode any new words. If they struggle, remind them to use a range of reading strategies, e.g. saying and blending letter sounds, reading root words before endings, deciding if the text makes sense, seeing a known word or sound within a word, using picture cues and developing basic inference and deduction skills.
- Ask questions to encourage these skills, e.g. *What can you do when you come to a word that you don't know?*

DURING READING

Independent reading:
- Encourage the children to read independently while you listen to each child in the group in turn.
- Model sounding out and blending, or ask individuals to decode words to the group.
- Point to the contractions *hadn't* and *didn't* and explain that the apostrophe represents the missing sound /o/.
- Highlight examples of successful problem-solving. Say: *You remembered the tricky word 'any'. Well done!*
- If appropriate, pause occasionally to reread a sentence, check for understanding and discuss the illustrations. Ask: *Why was Kangaroo in a hurry (on page 4)? Why did Koala apologise on page 6? How was Kangaroo feeling on page 13? Why do you think the friends went home slowly on page 15?*

AFTER READING

Return to the text:
- Share any words that caused difficulty with decoding, pronunciation or understanding.
- Explain why there are apostrophes in *Emu's nest* and *Spider's web*. The apostrophe shows us that the nest belongs to Emu and the web to Spider.
- Encourage the children to reflect on their learning. Ask: *How were Kangaroo and Koala feeling at the end of the story?*
- Use the comprehension questions at the end of the book to talk about the story and the main characters.
- Ask some of the following additional questions to check understanding of the story and explore the themes: *Do you think Koala was a good friend? Explain why. Why didn't Kangaroo notice the other animals? What do you think the other animals thought about Kangaroo? Do you know anyone who rushes around like Kangaroo?*

Follow-up activities:
1. Using the PCM provided, the children recall 'who said what' by writing the missing names next to the dialogue. Discuss why and how speech marks are used in the text.
2. Look through the story text to find words that are alternatives for 'said', e.g. *called, shouted*. Challenge the children to think of other examples, e.g. *yelled*, and identify places in the story where these could have been used.

BOOK OVERVIEW

One sunny morning, Koala is woken up by his energetic friend, Kangaroo, who is desperate to get to 'the big red rock'. Unfortunately, in her haste, Kangaroo is paying no attention to all the chaos she is causing on the way! Koala follows along behind his friend, putting things right and eventually saves Kangaroo from bouncing off the top of the rock!

Catch Up, Koala!

Name: _____ Date: _____

Who said what? Write the missing names.
You can use the book to help you.

"Wake up, Koala," said _____.

"Sorry," said _____.

"Look out for my eggs!" said _____.

"Look out for my web!" said _____.

"I was taking a nap!" said _____.

"Catch up, Koala," said _____.

Emu   Kangaroo   Koala   Spider   Lizard

AMAZING ANIMATION

Blue

GUIDED GROUP READING

BEFORE READING

Book introduction:

- Look together at the cover image, title and blurb of the book. Ask: *What is an 'animation'? Why are animations amazing?*
- Use flashcards or mini whiteboards to revise the following Blue letter/sound correspondences: wh, a-e ey a (long a), ea ey ie y e (long e), i-e y i (long i), ow o-e o (long o).
- Share and practise reading or sounding out the tricky words in this book: **animation, first, moving, pictures, our, animators, move, drawn, drew, people, watched, cinemas, around, before, Dinosaur, Walt, Mouse, minutes, Dwarfs, sound, colour, Alice, Wonderland, Beauty, Age, wanted, computer, use, Toy, Story.**
- Discuss the meaning of any unfamiliar words or phrases, such as: **flick, in black and white, steamboat, in colour.**

Strategy check:

- Encourage the children to use phonics skills to decode any new words. If they struggle, remind them to use a range of reading strategies, e.g. saying and blending letter sounds, reading root words before endings, deciding if the text makes sense, seeing a known word or sound within a word, using picture cues and developing basic inference and deduction skills.
- Ask questions to encourage these skills, e.g. *What can you do when you come to a word that you don't know?*

DURING READING

Independent reading:

- Encourage the children to read independently while you listen to each child in the group in turn.
- The children could read in pairs, reading two pages at a time to each other.
- Model sounding out and blending, or ask individuals to decode words to the group.
- Highlight examples of successful problem-solving. Say: *You recognised the long 'o' sound in 'most'. Well done!*
- If appropriate, pause occasionally to reread a sentence, check for understanding and discuss the illustrations. Ask: *Have you seen any of these animations before (on pages 2–3)? Which ones?*
Who was Walt Disney (on pages 8–9)?
What was special about 'Snow White and the Seven Dwarfs' (on page 10)?

AFTER READING

Return to the text:

- Share any words that caused difficulty with decoding, pronunciation or understanding, e.g. *cinema* where 'c' is pronounced /s/. Think of other examples: *circle, circus, centre.*
- Encourage the children to reflect on their learning. Ask: *Which came first: TVs or cartoons? Why is 'Toy Story' a special film?*
- Use the comprehension questions at the end of the book to talk about the cartoons featured and the children's favourite animations.
- Ask some of the following additional questions to check understanding of the text and explore the themes:
Why do you think the first cartoons were short?
Do you think it takes a lot of skill to make an animation? Explain why.
What skills does an animator need to have?
Why do you think the first animators drew on paper instead of using computers?

Follow-up activities:

1. Using the PCM provided, the children read the sentences and decide if they are true or false. They then link the book to their own experience by writing the name of their favourite cartoon, and why they like it.
2. Challenge the children to draw a (wordless) cartoon of their own, using pictures to tell a simple story. Tell them to base the storyline around one or two characters, at the most. Keep the ideas simple. Use comic books for inspiration.
3. As a class, research and explore how some animators use clay and modelling materials to make animations, rather than pen and paper. Have the children ever seen animations like these?

BOOK OVERVIEW

How does animation work and when was it invented? In this non-fiction book, the children learn all about the very first Mickey Mouse cartoons, created using paper drawings, and how modern animated films are now made using computers.

Amazing Animation

Name: _____ Date: _____

Read the sentences below. Circle 'True' if the sentence is true, or 'False' if the sentence is false. You can use the book to help you.

1. We can make pictures move by showing them at slow speed.   True   False

2. The first animated cartoons were silent.   True   False

3. Cartoons were invented before TVs.   True   False

4. Artists who draw moving cartoons are called 'animations'.   True   False

5. Mickey Mouse made the film 'Snow White and the Seven Dwarfs'.   True   False

What is your favourite cartoon?

My favourite cartoon is _____.

Why is it your favourite?

It is my favourite because _____.

VANYA THE VIKING

Blue

GUIDED GROUP READING

BEFORE READING

Book introduction:

- Look together at the cover image, title and blurb of the book. Ask: *Do you know what a Viking is? What type of story will this be?* (fiction, adventure)
- Use flashcards or mini whiteboards to revise the following Blue letter/sound correspondences: **wh, ay a-e a (long a), ea e-e y e (long e), i-e y i (long i), ow o-e o (long o)**.
- Share and practise reading or sounding out the tricky words in this book: **Viking, loves, doors, floors, aunt, coming, your, pulls, huge, wolf, wall, eyes, other, hero, new**.
- Discuss the meaning of any unfamiliar words or phrases, such as: **a waste of time, come in handy, elders**.

Strategy check:

- Encourage the children to use phonics skills to decode any new words. If they struggle, remind them to use a range of reading strategies, e.g. saying and blending letter sounds, reading root words before endings, deciding if the text makes sense, seeing a known word or sound within a word, using picture cues and developing basic inference and deduction skills.
- Ask questions to encourage these skills, e.g. *What can you do when you come to a word that you don't know?*

DURING READING

Independent reading:

- Encourage the children to read independently while you listen to each child in the group in turn.
- Remind the children to track underneath the words with their finger and to read all the words, including speech bubbles and sound effects.
- Model sounding out and blending, or ask individuals to decode words to the group.
- Highlight examples of successful problem-solving. Say: *You went back to the difficult word 'waste' after reading to the end of the sentence. Well done!*
- If appropriate, pause occasionally to reread a sentence, check for understanding and discuss the illustrations. Ask: *What is a skill (on page 4)? How do you think Vanya got the note (on page 6)? Why are the children howling (on pages 10–11)? Do you think Vanya likes her new job? (on page 15)?*

AFTER READING

Return to the text

- Share any words that caused difficulty with decoding, pronunciation or understanding.
- Encourage the children to reflect on their learning. Ask: *Why did Vanya's mum think painting was a waste of time? Do you think her mum changes her mind about Vanya's painting by the end of the story?*
- Use the comprehension questions at the end of the book to talk about the story and the success of Vanya's plan.
- Ask some of the following additional questions to check understanding of the book and explore the themes: *What does Vanya's mum mean by Viking skills? Who helped Vanya carry out her plan? Why did the robbers run away? Would you have drawn something different on the wall? Do you think Vanya will be a good teacher?*

Follow-up activities:

1. Using the PCM provided, review what the children observed and remembered about the story. Read the questions to the children. They then circle each correct answer.
2. Ask a group of children to act out a scene from the story, each playing a different character. Freeze-frame the group. Tap each character in turn and ask them to say what they are thinking or feeling.
3. Painting was Vanya's best skill. It made her happy. Ask the children: *What is your best skill?* Get the children to write a few sentences in answer to this question.

BOOK OVERVIEW

Vanya the Viking doesn't want to farm, sail or cook like all the other Vikings – she wants to paint! When she finds out robbers are on their way to steal all the sheep, Vanya puts a painting plan into action to scare them off. The robbers leave empty-handed and the village celebrates her skills by making her their art teacher!

Vanya the Viking

Name: _____ Date: _____

Read the questions. Circle each correct answer. You can use the book to help you.

1. Which of these is NOT a Viking skill?

   sailing   cooking   painting

2. Another word for 'robbers' is …

   elders   thieves   sheep

3. What colour were the wolf's eyes?

   bright green   bright blue   bright red

4. Why did the robbers run away?

   because they thought the wolf had eaten all the sheep

   because they thought Vanya had eaten all the sheep

   because they thought the Vikings had eaten all the sheep

5. At the end, the elders thought Vanya was …

   a hero   a teacher   a Viking

PLAY OUTSIDE

Blue

GUIDED GROUP READING

BEFORE READING

Book introduction:
- Look together at the cover image, title and blurb of the book. Ask: *What games do you like to play outside? Have you ever been on a woodland trail?*
- Use flashcards or mini whiteboards to revise the following Blue letter/sound correspondences: **wh, ay a-e a (long a), ea e-e y e (long e), i-e y i (long i), ow o-e o (long o)**.
- Share and practise reading or sounding out the tricky words in this book: **you're, outside, chalk, your, school, Monday, Tuesday, draw, picture, worms, whatever**.
- Discuss the meaning of any unfamiliar words or phrases, such as **bulb**.

Strategy check:
- Encourage the children to use phonics skills to decode any new words. If they struggle, remind them to use a range of reading strategies, e.g. saying and blending letter sounds, reading root words before endings, deciding if the text makes sense, seeing a known word or sound within a word, using picture cues and developing basic inference and deduction skills.
- Ask questions to encourage these skills, e.g. *What can you do when you come to a word that you don't know?*

DURING READING

Independent reading:
- Encourage the children to read independently while you listen to each child in the group in turn.
- Remind the children to track underneath the words with their finger and to read all the words, as some text appears in different places on the page.
- Model sounding out and blending, or ask individuals to decode words to the group.
- Highlight examples of successful problem-solving. Say: *You read the contraction 'you're' perfectly. Well done!*
- If appropriate, pause occasionally to reread a sentence, check for understanding and discuss the illustrations. Ask: *Do you see traffic lights on your way home (on page 5)?*
What was the weather like on Monday (on page 7)?
Which animals can you see on page 9?
Do you know any other games you can play with chalk (on page 13)?
How do you make a sand animal (on page 14)?

AFTER READING

Return to the text:
- Share any words that caused difficulty with decoding, pronunciation or understanding. Break down *Saturday* into syllables (*Sat/ur/day*) to help with decoding.
- Ask the children which letter/sounds are missing in the contractions *you're* and *what's*.
- Encourage the children to reflect on their learning. Ask: *Can you play outside in all weathers? Do you need equipment to play outside?*
- Use the comprehension questions at the end of the book to talk about the text and the games children play outside.
- Ask some of the following additional questions to check understanding of the book and explore the themes:
What games have you played outside today?
What could you play outside when it's snowing?
Do you know an activity you could do outside when it's windy?
Have you ever made anything outside that you were proud of?

Follow-up activities:
1. Using the PCM provided, the children recall information from the book by drawing lines to match words taken from the book to the pictures. They can then write about things they would like to find on a nature trail.
2. Turn to pages 8–9 in the book. Ask the children what they can see outside their home. They can draw a picture and write matching word labels, e.g. *tree, house, cars, road,* etc.

BOOK OVERVIEW

What activities can we play outside? This book provides plenty of fun ideas for interesting things the children can do, and games they can play outside with simple items they find around them.

Play Outside

Name: _____ Date: _____

Draw lines to match the words to the items you might find on a nature trail.

leaves

flower

pine cone

bark

feather

worm

spider

animal tracks

What would you like to find on a nature trail?

I would like to find _____.

RUMPELSTILTSKIN

Green

GUIDED GROUP READING

BEFORE READING

Book introduction:
- Look together at the cover image, title and blurb of the book. Ask: *What type of book do you think this is? (fiction, fairy tale) Can we always trust people who offer to help us?*
- Use flashcards or mini whiteboards to revise the following Green letter/sound correspondences: **ew** (long u), **ue u** (/y+oo/), **u ou oul** (short oo), **ir er ear or** (/er/), **ere** (/air/), **au our augh ore oor** (/or/).
- Share and practise reading or sounding out the tricky words in this book: **prince, love, you're, meant, necklace, choice, demanded, guess, Rumpelstiltskin**.
- Discuss the meaning of any unfamiliar words or phrases, such as: **miller, promise**.

Strategy check:
- Encourage the children to use phonics skills to decode any new words. If they struggle, remind them to use a range of reading strategies, e.g. saying and blending letter sounds, reading root words before endings, deciding if the text makes sense, seeing a known word or sound within a word, using picture cues and developing basic inference and deduction skills.
- Ask questions to encourage these skills, e.g. *What can you do when you come to a word that you don't know?*

DURING READING

Independent reading:
- Encourage the children to read independently while you listen to each child in the group in turn.
- When reading aloud, the children could try to use different voices for different characters.
- Model sounding out and blending, or ask individuals to decode words to the group.
- Highlight examples of successful problem-solving. Say: *You correctly predicted the word 'promise' by thinking about the words that came before it. Well done!*
- If appropriate, pause occasionally to reread a sentence, check for understanding and discuss the illustrations. Ask: *What words would you use to describe the king's actions on page 7? Why did Lara have no choice (on page 10)? Why did the little man come back (on page 12)?*

AFTER READING

Return to the text:
- Share any words that caused difficulty with decoding, pronunciation or understanding.
- Encourage the children to reflect on their learning. Ask: *Where do you think Rumpelstiltskin goes at the end of the story? Do you think he will come back one day?*
- Use the comprehension questions at the end of the book to talk about the story and the main characters: Rumpelstiltskin and Lara.
- Ask some of the following additional questions to check understanding of the story and explore the themes: *How would you describe Rumpelstiltskin? Have you ever made a promise you couldn't keep? Fairy tales often begin with the words 'Once upon a time…'. What words do they usually end with?*

Follow-up activities:
1. Using the PCM provided, the children practise their reading and sequencing skills by cutting out the sentences and sorting them into the correct order. Encourage the children to refer back to the book if they wish.
2. The king, Lara and Rumpelstiltskin all made promises to each other in the story. Ask the children: *Have you ever made a promise? What was it and did you keep it?* Encourage the children to share their experiences.
3. Challenge the children to create a new rhyme for Rumpelstiltskin on page 17. As a class, first make a list of rhyming words to help with ideas and spelling.

BOOK OVERVIEW

The prince wants to marry Lara, the miller's daughter, but the king refuses unless she can spin wheat into gold. Luckily for Lara, Rumpelstiltskin promises to help her, but only in return for her firstborn child. Lara reluctantly agrees and the prince and Lara are finally married. Later, when Rumpelstiltskin returns, Lara discovers a secret that will save the child.

Rumpelstiltskin

Name: _____ Date: _____

Cut out the sentences. Put them in the order they appear in the story. You can use the book to help you.

✂

The king kept his promise and Lara married Prince Roberto.

"I'll give you anything but my son."

On that last night, Lara followed the little man home.

Once upon a time, a prince fell in love with a miller's daughter.

Lara and Roberto looked up all the names in the land.

"I will turn this wheat into gold if you give me your necklace," he said.

He vanished in a puff of smoke.

Reading Planet Galaxy © Rising Stars UK Ltd 2018. You may photocopy this page.

TOYS FROM 100 YEARS AGO

Green

GUIDED GROUP READING

BEFORE READING

Book introduction:

- Look together at the cover image, title and blurb of the book. Ask: *What date was it 100 years ago? Do you know anyone who is 100 years old?*
- Use flashcards or mini whiteboards to revise the following Green letter/sound correspondences: **ew u-e (long u), u (/y+oo/), u ou (short oo), ir er ear or (/er/), ere are (/air/), aw al augh ore (/or/)**.
- Share and practise reading or sounding out the tricky words in this book: **Meccano®, tricycle, uncle, move, horsehair, aunt, tyre, palace, castle**.
- Discuss the meaning of any unfamiliar words or phrases, such as: **discover, motor, wound up, oval**.

Strategy check:

- Encourage the children to use phonics skills to decode any new words. If they struggle, remind them to use a range of reading strategies, e.g. saying and blending letter sounds, reading root words before endings, deciding if the text makes sense, seeing a known word or sound within a word, using picture cues and developing basic inference and deduction skills.
- Ask questions to encourage these skills, e.g. *What can you do when you come to a word that you don't know?*

DURING READING

Independent reading:

- Encourage the children to read independently while you listen to each child in the group in turn.
- Remind the children to read all the words on the page, including any captions and labels.
- Model sounding out and blending, or ask individuals to decode words to the group.
- Highlight examples of successful problem-solving. Say: *You split the word 'clockwork' into two words to read it. Well done!*
- If appropriate, pause occasionally to reread a sentence, check for understanding and discuss the illustrations. Ask: *Who gave Harry the humming top (on page 5)? What would you find in a Meccano® kit (pages 10–11)? Do children play with train sets like this today (on page 12)?*

AFTER READING

Return to the text:

- Share any words that caused difficulty with decoding, pronunciation or understanding.
- Encourage the children to reflect on their learning. Ask: *Whose toys were shown in the book? Are any of the toys in this book still popular today?*
- Use the comprehension questions at the end of the book to talk about the text and why the toys in the book were popular.
- Ask some of the following additional questions to check understanding of the book and explore the themes:
Do you think you need a lot of skill to play Blow Football?
Do children still ride tricycles today?
Have you ever seen or played with a dolls' house?
Which of these toys looks the most fun? Explain why.
Have you ever written a thank you note? Who was it to and why did you write it?

Follow-up activities:

1. Using the PCM provided, the children draw a picture of one of their own toys, then practise composition by writing a thank-you note to the person (or people) who gave them this toy.
2. Ask the children to draw pictures or cut pictures out of magazines to create a class poster of popular toys from the past and popular toys today. Compare the toys. Ask: *In what ways are they different/the same?*

BOOK OVERVIEW

Have toys changed in the last 100 years? Travel back in time to take a look at popular toys from 1924: a spinning top, a tricycle, Blow Football and a Meccano® set. The best gift of all is Queen Mary's dolls' house, which she shared with the people of Great Britain, and which is still on display at Windsor Castle.

Toys From 100 Years Ago

Name: _____ Date: _____

Draw a picture of one of your toys.
Write a thank you note to the person (or people) who bought it for you to say what you like about it.
Use some of the words below or choose your own.

with	for	much
toy	thank	you
play	very	like
my	present	

Dear: _____

_____

_____

_____

_____

From: _____

SOPHIE GOES TO THE BALLET

Green

GUIDED GROUP READING

BEFORE READING

Book introduction:
- Look together at the cover image, title and blurb of the book. Ask: *What is 'the ballet'? Have you ever seen someone performing ballet?*
- Use flashcards or mini whiteboards to revise the following Green letter/sound correspondences: **u-e (long u), u (/y+oo/), u ou (short oo), ir er ear or (/er/), ere (/air/), aw al oor (/or/).**
- Share and practise reading or sounding out the tricky words in this book: **excited, ballet, theatre, huge, above, chandelier, pieces, performance, stage, musicians, ready, orchestra, exciting, dancers, magical, characters, ice-cream, scenery, breath.**
- Discuss the meaning of any unfamiliar words or phrases, such as: **velvet, dimmed, the first act, took her breath away.**

Strategy check:
- Encourage the children to use phonics skills to decode any new words. If they struggle, remind them to use a range of reading strategies, e.g. saying and blending letter sounds, reading root words before endings, deciding if the text makes sense, seeing a known word or sound within a word, using picture cues and developing basic inference and deduction skills.
- Ask questions to encourage these skills, e.g. *What can you do when you come to a word that you don't know?*

DURING READING

Independent reading:
- Encourage the children to read independently while you listen to each child in the group in turn.
- Model sounding out and blending, or ask individuals to decode words to the group.
- Highlight examples of successful problem-solving. Say: *I like the way you sounded out the word 'performance'. Well done!*
- If appropriate, pause occasionally to reread a sentence, check for understanding and discuss the illustrations.
Ask: *Why did the bell ring (on page 9)?*
Why did Sophie say, "I was wrong." (on page 11)?
What was the most beautiful thing Sophie had ever seen on page 14?
What was the 'interval' (on page 16)?

AFTER READING

Return to the text:
- Share any words that caused difficulty with decoding, pronunciation or understanding.
- Encourage the children to reflect on their learning. Ask: *Why did Sophie's gran take her to the ballet? Did Sophie want to be a dancer when she grew up?*
- Use the comprehension questions at the end of the book to talk about the story and the children's experiences of visiting a theatre.
- Ask some of the following additional questions to check understanding of the story and explore the themes:
Was the performance in the daytime or the evening?
Can you remember what the huge, sparkling light was called?
What was in the book that Gran bought?
Do you think Sophie would like to go to the ballet again? Explain why.
Does Sophie like ice-cream? Say why.

Follow-up activities:
1. Using the PCM provided, the children practise descriptive writing by pretending they are Sophie and writing about her trip to the ballet. They can use phrases from the vocabulary box.
2. As a group, create a list of words to describe movements made by a dancer, for example: spin, twist, twirl, hop. Encourage the children to come up with some alliterative phrases using these words, for example: *he twists and twirls, she spins and skips*.

BOOK OVERVIEW

Sophie's grandmother is taking her to see the ballet for the very first time. Everything Sophie sees is new and exciting but the dancers on stage are the best and take her breath away!

Sophie Goes to the Ballet

Name: _____ Date: _____

Imagine you are Sophie. Write about the trip to the ballet. Use the words from the box below to help you.

Today _____.

It was _____.

and _____.

I would like to go again because _____
_____.

went   ballet   most   beautiful   thing   seen
wonderful   amazing   ever   spectacular
brilliant   exciting   fun   interesting

MY SUPER SENSES

Green

GUIDED GROUP READING

BEFORE READING

Book introduction:
- Look together at the cover image, title and blurb of the book. Ask: *What are your senses? Why are they 'super'?*
- Use flashcards or mini whiteboards to revise the following Green letter/sound correspondences: **ew u-e** (long u), **u** (/y+oo/), **u ou** (short oo), **er ear or** (/er/), **ou** (/ear/), **ere** (/air/), **aw al our** (/or/).
- Share and practise reading or sounding out the tricky words in this book: **scientists, picture, quiet, guess, tongue, onion, rough, questions, experiments**.
- Discuss the meaning of any unfamiliar words or phrases, such as: **scientists, dab**.

Strategy check:
- Encourage the children to use phonics skills to decode any new words. If they struggle, remind them to use a range of reading strategies, e.g. saying and blending letter sounds, reading root words before endings, deciding if the text makes sense, seeing a known word or sound within a word, using picture cues and developing basic inference and deduction skills.
- Ask questions to encourage these skills, e.g. *What can you do when you come to a word that you don't know?*

DURING READING

Independent reading:
- Encourage the children to read independently while you listen to each child in the group in turn.
- Remind the children to read all the text, including headings, captions and charts.
- Model sounding out and blending, or ask individuals to decode words to the group.
- Highlight examples of successful problem-solving. Say: *You recognised the silent letter in 'guess'. Well done!*
- If appropriate, pause after each page to reread the sentence, check for understanding and discuss the illustrations. Ask: *Why do we see this picture differently (on pages 4–5)?*
Did everyone guess lemon correctly (on page 11)?
Which taste did the children like the least (on page 13)?
Which food did all five children guess correctly without smelling it (on page 15)?

AFTER READING

Return to the text:
- Share any words that caused difficulty with decoding, pronunciation or understanding.
- Encourage the children to reflect on their learning. Ask: *Do you think your senses are super? Say why. Which sense would you like to learn more about?*
- Use the comprehension questions at the end of the book to talk about the text and how our senses help us.
- Ask some of the following additional questions to check understanding of the book and explore the themes:
How many senses do we have?
Would food taste different if you didn't have a sense of smell?
Which fact from this book did you find the most interesting?
Do you think we need all of our senses?

Follow-up activities:
1. Using the PCM provided, the children recall details from the text by cutting out the sentences and sticking them around the character. They then draw lines from the sentences to the correct parts of the body.
2. Support children to carry out some of the senses experiments found in the reader.
3. As a class, research animal senses. Any children who have pets may be interested to find out about their pets' senses. Ask: *How are animals' senses different/ the same? Are they better than our (human) senses?* The children write sentences about the similarities and differences.

BOOK OVERVIEW

How good is our sense of smell? Can sound travel through string? Which taste do people like best? This non-fiction book answers all of these questions through simple experiments to help the children understand how their super senses work!

My Super Senses

Name: _____ Date: _____

Cut out the sentences below.
Stick them around the picture.
Draw lines from the sentences to the correct parts of the body.

✂

You see with your eyes.	You hear with your ears.
You smell with your nose.	You taste with your mouth.
You feel with your skin.	

BILLY BUILDS SOMETHING BIG

Green

GUIDED GROUP READING

BEFORE READING

Book introduction:

- Look together at the cover image, title and blurb of the book. Ask: *What could 'something big' be? Have you ever built anything big?*
- Use flashcards or mini whiteboards to revise the following Green letter/sound correspondences: **ew ue u-e (long u), ue u-e u (/y+oo/), u ou oul (short oo), er ear or (/er/), ere ear (/air/), aw al au our ore (/or/).**
- Share and practise reading or sounding out the tricky words in this book: **busy, build, space, thought, moved, field, building, world, built, huge, place, sure.**
- Discuss the meaning of any unfamiliar words or phrases, such as: **hardly, sanded, smoothed, waxed, launched.**

Strategy check:

- Encourage the children to use phonics skills to decode any new words. If they struggle, remind them to use a range of reading strategies, e.g. saying and blending letter sounds, reading root words before endings, deciding if the text makes sense, seeing a known word or sound within a word, using picture cues and developing basic inference and deduction skills.
- Ask questions to encourage these skills, e.g. *What can you do when you come to a word that you don't know?*

DURING READING

Independent reading:

- Encourage the children to read independently while you listen to each child in the group in turn.
- Model sounding out and blending, or ask individuals to decode words to the group.
- Draw attention to the alliteration in the text: *bits and bobs; he sanded and stuck and smoothed.*
- Highlight examples of successful problem-solving. Say: *I like the way you broke down the word 'actually' into parts to decode it. Well done!*
- If appropriate, pause occasionally to reread a sentence, check for understanding and discuss the illustrations. Ask: *What might people in the park be thinking (on page 7)? Where do you think Billy is going to keep it next (on page 13)?*

AFTER READING

Return to the text:

- Share any words that caused difficulty with decoding, pronunciation or understanding.
- Choose text from the book and talk about how adding -ed to verbs changes the sentence.
- Encourage the children to reflect on their learning. Ask: *Can you think of words to describe Billy's character? (creative, clever, hard-working) Do you think Billy's planet will become famous?*
- Use the comprehension questions at the end of the book to talk about the story and big building projects in your locality/town.
- Ask some of the following additional questions to check understanding of the book and explore the themes: *Why didn't Billy play football at the beginning of the story? What do you think it would be like to play football on Billy's planet? Have you ever visited a huge building? What was it like? Do you think Billy will build anything else in the future?*

Follow-up activities:

1. Using the PCM provided, the children recall details from the story by deciding whether statements about Billy's big build are true or false. They then write a correct sentence for those marked false. They can refer to the reader text to help them.
2. Get the children to role-play the part of Billy and a news reporter, who is interviewing Billy about his big build. Help them to think of suitable interview questions, e.g. *What materials did you use? How long did the build take?* Tell the children to use ideas from the book for Billy's responses.

BOOK OVERVIEW

Billy has no time or space to play football with his friends – he is building something big in his shed! Billy's project quickly increases in size so he has to move it from one bigger location to the next – from the countryside to the South Pole! Finally, Billy's now 'something huge' ends up in space – it's a brand-new planet to play football on!

Billy Builds Something Big

Name: _____ Date: _____

Are these sentences true or false? Circle the correct answer. Write a correct sentence for those marked false. You can use the book to help you.

1. Billy was going to build something small. True   False

   _____

2. Billy's something big was too big for the garden. True   False

   _____

3. The whole world was delighted. True   False

   _____

4. Billy launched his something huge into the sea. True   False

   _____

5. Billy played football in space. True   False

   _____

MY NATURE ACTIVITY BOOK

Green

GUIDED GROUP READING

BEFORE READING

Book introduction:
- Look together at the cover image, title and blurb of the book. Ask: *What is 'nature'? Have you ever been on a nature walk?*
- Use flashcards or mini whiteboards to revise the following Green letter/sound correspondences: **ew ue u-e (long u), ue u-e u (/y+oo/), u ou (short oo), ir er ear or (/er/), ere (/air/), aw al our ore (/or/)**.
- Share and practise reading or sounding out the tricky words in this book: **nature, hedgehog, pieces, head, pebbles, fruit, ice-lolly, middle, sugar, mixture, distance, sprinkle, spread**.
- Discuss the meaning of any unfamiliar words or phrases, such as: **lurking, damp**.

Strategy check:
- Encourage the children to use phonics skills to decode any new words. If they struggle, remind them to use a range of reading strategies, e.g. saying and blending letter sounds, reading root words before endings, deciding if the text makes sense, seeing a known word or sound within a word, using picture cues and developing basic inference and deduction skills.
- Ask questions to encourage these skills, e.g. *What can you do when you come to a word that you don't know?*

DURING READING

Independent reading:
- Encourage the children to read independently while you listen to each child in the group in turn.
- Model sounding out and blending, or ask individuals to decode words to the group.
- Highlight examples of successful problem-solving. Say: *I like the way you broke down the compound word 'sometimes' into separate words to decode it. Well done!*
- If appropriate, pause occasionally to reread a sentence, check for understanding and discuss the illustrations. Ask: *What are minibeasts (on page 2)? How do new pine trees grow (on page 4)? How do you make the hedgehog's nose (on page 5)? Where has the pattern on the rubbing come from (on page 9)? Why do you think bees get tired (on page 12)?*

AFTER READING

Return to the text:
- Share any words that caused difficulty with decoding, pronunciation or understanding.
- Challenge the children to find compound words in the text, e.g. *hedgehog, ladybirds, bookmark, eggshell, eggcup, teaspoon, windowsill, cardboard,* etc.
- Encourage the children to reflect on their learning. Ask: *How can we identify different trees? What interesting fact have you learned from this book that you didn't already know?*
- Use the comprehension questions at the end of the book to talk about the text, and the trees and wildlife in your local area.
- Ask some of the following additional questions to check understanding of the book and explore the themes: *What types of trees grow in our local area? What do bees like to eat? Why do birds need extra food in winter? How can we help wildlife in our local area?*

Follow-up activities:
1. Using the PCM provided, the children draw lines to match materials from the book with items that can be made from them. They then link to their own experience by ticking boxes to show what they have seen on nature walks.
2. Go on a nature walk at school. Try to identify some common trees, flowers and minibeasts. Ask the children to draw sketches and take photographs. Create a classroom display from your findings.
3. Ask the children: *How can we help the wildlife in our local area/school grounds?* Challenge them, in pairs, to come up with ideas for a wildlife-friendly garden, for example: bee-friendly flowers, homemade bird boxes, insect shelters, etc.

BOOK OVERVIEW

In this non-fiction book, the children explore what they might find on a nature walk and how these items can be used for interesting and useful craft projects. They also find out ways to help and conserve wildlife.

My Nature Activity Book

Name: _____   Date: _____

Draw lines to show what you can make with each material. You can use the book to help you.

Materials	**What you can make**
pine cones	a snack for birds
pebbles	an egghead
tree trunks	a drink for bees
ice-lolly stick and paper	flower bookmarks
sugar and water	tree rubbings
eggshell and cress	hedgehogs
a cardboard tube, honey and seeds	paint them to look like bees or ladybirds

(pine cones — hedgehogs)

What other things can we see on a nature walk? Tick the box next to the things you have seen.

leaves ☐   flowers ☐

conkers ☐   a log ☐

twigs ☐   birds ☐

ROBIN HOOD AND THE GOLDEN ARROW

Orange

GUIDED GROUP READING

BEFORE READING

Book introduction:
- Look together at the cover image, title and blurb of the book. Ask: *Who is Robin Hood? When/where does the story take place?*
- Use flashcards or mini whiteboards to revise the following Orange letter/sound correspondences: **ce cy st** (/s/), **ge dge** (/j/), **le, kn, tch, ture, tion** (/sh/), **ea** (/e/), **(w)a,** (/o/).
- Share and practise reading or sounding out the tricky words in this book: **Nottingham, competition, villager, money, prisoner, soldiers, captured, disappeared, wounded, dungeons, guard, drawbridge, disappeared.**
- Discuss the meaning of any unfamiliar words or phrases, such as: **took aim, captor, cell, swiftly, turret.**

Strategy check:
- Encourage the children to use phonics skills to decode any new words. If they struggle, remind them to use a range of reading strategies, e.g. saying and blending letter sounds, reading root words before endings, deciding if the text makes sense, seeing a known word or sound within a word, using picture cues and developing basic inference and deduction skills.
- Ask questions to encourage these skills, e.g. *What can you do when you come to a word that you don't know?*

DURING READING

Independent reading:
- Encourage the children to read independently while you listen to each child in the group in turn.
- Some children could read in pairs, taking turns to read a page to each other.
- When reading aloud, the children could try to use different voices for different characters.
- Highlight examples of successful problem-solving. Say: *You correctly pronounced the letters 'ce' in 'noticed' as /s/. Well done!*
- If appropriate, pause after each page to reread the sentence, check for understanding and discuss the illustrations. Ask: *Why does Robin say it would serve the Sheriff right on page 5? Why were they bringing buckets of water up from the moat on page 14? What do you think will happen next (on page 15)?*

AFTER READING

Return to the text:
- Share any words that caused difficulty with decoding, pronunciation or understanding.
- Identify the root words in past-tense verbs, e.g. <u>point</u>ed, <u>laugh</u>ed, <u>pull</u>ed.
- Encourage the children to reflect on their learning. Ask: *Did the story end well for all the characters? Did the Sheriff's trick work out as he hoped it would?*
- Use the comprehension questions at the end of the book to talk about the story and the main characters: Robin Hood and the Sheriff.
- Ask some of the following additional questions to check understanding of the book and explore the themes:
Why does the Sheriff hate Robin?
Do you think the villagers like the Sheriff? Explain your answer.
Do the villagers like Robin? Say why.
Have you ever visited a castle like the one in the story? What did you like about it?

Follow-up activities:
1. Using the PCM provided, the children practise using verbs by inserting the missing words into the sentences from the book.
2. Ask a group of children to each choose a different sentence from the book and draw a picture to illustrate it. The children write the sentence below the picture. Then, together as a group, try to put the sentences in the correct order.

BOOK OVERVIEW

Robin Hood is persuaded to take part in the Sheriff of Nottingham's archery competition, to win a golden arrow. However, Robin quickly discovers that the competition is a trick to lure and capture him and his friends. Thankfully, clever Robin has a plan up his sleeve to free his friends and take the prize!

Robin Hood and the Golden Arrow

Name: _____ Date: _____

Add in the missing action words to the sentences. You can use the book to help you.

1. Robin _____ carefully as the arrow flew.

2. He _____ the arrow out of the air.

3. "_____ you!" he _____.

4. Robin and his friends _____ into the forest.

5. "Thank you, Robin!" they _____.

tricked   cheered   disappeared
shouted   snatched   watched

INCREDIBLE CREATURES FROM GREEK MYTHS

Orange

GUIDED GROUP READING

BEFORE READING

Book introduction:
- Look together at the cover image, title and blurb of the book. Ask: *What is a Greek myth? Do you know where Greece is?*
- Ask if any of the children have ever visited Greece.
- Use flashcards or mini whiteboards to revise the following Orange letter/sound correspondences: **ch** (/k/), **ce cy sc** (/s/), **ge gi** (/j/), **le, kn, wr, ture, tion** (/sh/), **ea** (/e/), **(w)a,** (/o/), **y** (/i/).
- Share and practise reading or sounding out the tricky words in this book: **soldiers, woman, women, answer, fought, breathe**.
- Discuss the meaning of any unfamiliar words or phrases, such as: **riddle**.

Strategy check:
- Encourage the children to use phonics skills to decode any new words. If they struggle, remind them to use a range of reading strategies, e.g. saying and blending letter sounds, reading root words before endings, deciding if the text makes sense, seeing a known word or sound within a word, using picture cues and developing basic inference and deduction skills.
- Ask questions to encourage these skills, e.g. *What can you do when you come to a word that you don't know?*

DURING READING

Independent reading:
- Encourage the children to read independently while you listen to each child in the group in turn.
- Some children could read in pairs, taking turns to read a double page to each other.
- Model sounding out and blending, or ask individuals to decode words to the group.
- Highlight examples of successful problem-solving. Say: *The word 'lead' can be pronounced in different ways for different meanings. Well done!*
- If appropriate, pause occasionally to reread a sentence, check for understanding and discuss the illustrations. Ask: *Why does the Sphinx look shocked on page 7? How do you think Pegasus could have helped to beat the Chimera (on page 12)? What do you think Chiron is saying to the men on page 16?*

AFTER READING

Return to the text:
- Share any words that caused difficulty with decoding, pronunciation or understanding, e.g. we don't pronounce the 'o' in *Oedipus*.
- Challenge the children to find words ending in the suffix *-ture*, e.g. adventure, creature. Do they know any others? (capture, nature)
- Encourage the children to reflect on their learning. Ask: *Which is your favourite mythical creature from the book? Say why. Were all the beasts cruel and scary?*
- Use the comprehension questions at the end of the book to talk about the text, and the amazing creatures and heroes from Greek myths.
- Ask some of the following additional questions to check understanding of the book and explore the themes: *Which beast was the scariest on the beast-o-meter? Which creature was wise and kind? Can you remember the names of any Greek heroes? Which Greek creatures can we see in the stars?*

Follow-up activities:
1. Using the PCM provided, the children revise vocabulary from the book by writing the missing names of the creatures to complete the sentences. They then draw their own mythical creature and give it a name. Use this opportunity to remind the children that names begin with capital letters.
2. The Sphinx was the beast who ate anyone who couldn't answer her riddle (see pages 6–7). Challenge the children, in pairs, to invent a riddle for others to answer. Ask: *Which of you will escape the Sphinx?*

BOOK OVERVIEW

Which beasts from the Greek myths were good and which ones were very bad? This simple introduction to some of Greek mythology's well-known creatures includes a summary of each character, and a 'beast-o-meter' to measure their beastly qualities!

Incredible Creatures from Greek Myths

Name: _____ Date: _____

Write the missing names of the creatures to complete the sentences below. Remember to use a capital letter to start each name. Use the book to check your answers!

The white horse with wings was _____.

The _____ ate anyone who couldn't answer her riddle.

The huge giant with one eye was _____.

The _____ was trapped in the world's biggest maze.

_____ had wriggling snakes for hair.

The _____ was a fire-breathing monster.

Minotaur   Chimera   Medusa   Cyclops   Sphinx   Pegasus

Draw your own mythical creature and give it a name!

THE SAMURAI'S BRAVE DAUGHTER

Orange

GUIDED GROUP READING

BEFORE READING

Book introduction:
- Look together at the cover image, title and blurb of the book. Ask: *What do you think Tokoyo will do to show she is brave? When/where do you think this story takes place?*
- Talk about the job of the Samurai in protecting the Japanese Emperor.
- Use flashcards or mini whiteboards to revise the following Orange letter/sound correspondences: **ce ci** (/s/), **ge** (/j/), **le, kn, wr, tion** (/sh/), **ea** (/e/), **(w)a,** (/o/).
- Share and practise reading or sounding out the tricky words in this book: **Tokoyo, guards, island, towards, scary, dangerous, move**.
- Discuss the meaning of any unfamiliar words or phrases, such as: **warrior, loomed, sprang**.

Strategy check:
- Encourage the children to use phonics skills to decode any new words. If they struggle, remind them to use a range of reading strategies, e.g. saying and blending letter sounds, reading root words before endings, deciding if the text makes sense, seeing a known word or sound within a word, using picture cues and developing basic inference and deduction skills.
- Ask questions to encourage these skills, e.g. *What can you do when you come to a word that you don't know?*

DURING READING

Independent reading:
- Encourage the children to read independently while you listen to each child in the group in turn.
- Some children could read in pairs, taking turns to read a page to each other.
- Highlight examples of successful problem-solving. Say: *You correctly pronounced the letters 'ce' as /s/ in 'celebrating'. Well done!*
- If appropriate, pause occasionally to reread a sentence, check for understanding and discuss the illustrations. Ask: *Was the Emperor right to send Tokoyo's father away (on page 4)? How does Tokoyo fight the Sea-Dragon without a weapon (on pages 14–15)? How do you think Tokoyo is feeling on page 16?*

AFTER READING

Return to the text:
- Share any words that caused difficulty with decoding, pronunciation or understanding.
- Tokoyo is described as brave in the book title. Challenge the children to think of other words to describe her, e.g. clever, fast, skilful.
- Encourage the children to reflect on their learning. Ask: *Did the story end well for all the characters? Would you like to have lived in Tokoyo's world? Say why.*
- Use the comprehension questions at the end of the book to talk about the story and Tokoyo's bravery.
- Ask some of the following additional questions to check understanding of the book and explore the themes: *Why did the villagers leave food for the sea-dragon? Why did the Emperor change his mind about Tokoyo's father? Do you think the Sea Dragon will come back? Why/why not? What was the job of the Samurai warriors? Do you need to be brave to be a Samurai? Why?*

Follow-up activities:
1. Using the PCM provided, the children use what they have learned from the story to write character descriptions of Tokoyo and the Emperor.
2. Ask the children to reread the story and find examples of Tokoyo's brave behaviour, e.g. she left the palace and went to look for her father; she fought the Sea Dragon and won.
3. Ask the children to write or talk about a time when they have had to show bravery.

BOOK OVERVIEW

After an Emperor banishes one of his Samurai guards in error, Tokoyo, the guard's brave daughter, goes to find her father. As she reaches the coast, she encounters some villagers who are very afraid of a terrible Sea Dragon. The only person who could defeat such a beast is a Samurai. Tokoyo takes on the dragon and wins. Word of her bravery reaches the Emperor who pardons her father and takes her on as one of his own Samurai guards.

The Samurai's Brave Daughter

Name: _____   Date: _____

Write character descriptions of Tokoyo and the Emperor. You can use the word bank below to help you.

Tokoyo

_____

_____

_____

_____

The Emperor

_____

_____

_____

_____

| brave | warrior | angry | clever |
| fast | kind | wrong | sorry |

RICHARD AND THE LIONS

Orange

GUIDED GROUP READING
BEFORE READING

Book introduction:
- Look together at the cover image, title and blurb of the book. Ask: *Could this be a true story? Where do you think this story takes place?*
- Use flashcards or mini whiteboards to revise the following Orange letter/sound correspondences: **ch** (/k/), **ce ci cy** (/s/), **ge** (/j/), **le**, **tch**, **tion** (/sh/), **(w)a**, (/o/), **y** (/i/).
- Share and practise reading or sounding out the tricky words in this book: **Nairobi, discovered, moving, radio, idea, group, hyenas, leopards, buildings, together**.
- Discuss the meaning of any unfamiliar words or phrases, such as: **cattle, hides, spare parts**.

Strategy check:
- Encourage the children to use phonics skills to decode any new words. If they struggle, remind them to use a range of reading strategies, e.g. saying and blending letter sounds, reading root words before endings, deciding if the text makes sense, seeing a known word or sound within a word, using picture cues and developing basic inference and deduction skills.
- Ask questions to encourage these skills, e.g. *What can you do when you come to a word that you don't know?*

DURING READING

Independent reading:
- Encourage the children to read independently while you listen to each child in the group in turn.
- Some children could read in pairs, taking turns to read a page to each other.
- Talk about the page headings, labels and glossary.
- Highlight examples of successful problem-solving. Say: *You correctly sounded out the 'y' in the word 'hyenas' as /igh/. Well done!*
- If appropriate, pause occasionally to reread a sentence, check for understanding and discuss the illustrations. Ask: *Do you think Richard was happy to go to school (on page 15)? Why/why not?*
Would people still be interested if the lights had been expensive (on page 16)?
Why does Richard no longer hate lions (on page 18)?
Which of the items in the glossary were used to make Richard's lights (on page 19)?

AFTER READING

Return to the text:
- Share any words that caused difficulty with decoding, pronunciation or understanding.
- Challenge the children to add more words to the glossary, e.g. *Maasai*.
- Encourage the children to reflect on their learning. Ask: *What was Richard's invention? How did he save the cattle and the lions?*
- Use the comprehension questions at the end of the book to talk about the text and how Richard's lion lights changed people's lives for the better.
- Ask some of the following additional questions to check understanding of the book and explore the themes:
How did Richard know how to make electric lights?
How did Richard's idea make a difference to people's lives?
How did he save other animals, as well as lions?
What job do you think Richard would enjoy when he's older?

Follow-up activities:
1. Using the PCM provided, children recall vocabulary from the book by drawing lines to match the words to the correct glossary definitions. They can then check their answers in the book.
2. Discuss what an inventor is. Together with the children, try to identify examples of inventions that have changed people's lives, e.g. motor car, computer. Make a 'Great Inventions' list or a poster from your ideas.

BOOK OVERVIEW

In this book, the children learn how young Maasai boy, Richard Turere, solved a huge problem for his people when he invented a cheap way to prevent lions attacking their cattle. Richard's invention has not only benefited the Maasai people, but also prevented different species of African wildlife from being killed. Richard is the youngest person to hold a patent in Kenya for his Lion Lights.

Richard and the Lions

Name: _____ Date: _____

Work out the words from the glossary and then draw lines to join them to the correct definitions on the right.

dung — animal skin

electrical wire — something that makes electricity when the Sun's rays shine on it

solar panel — a switch to make a light flash on and off

scarecrow — animal poo

hide — a model of a person in old clothes, used to scare animals

indicator box — a metal wire for joining lights and switches to a battery

Reading Planet Galaxy © Rising Stars UK Ltd 2018. You may photocopy this page.

THE JUMPY BUMPY FEELING

Orange

GUIDED GROUP READING

BEFORE READING

Book introduction:
- Look together at the cover image, title and blurb of the book. Ask: *When have you felt a 'jumpy bumpy' feeling inside? Can you think of other words to replace 'jumpy bumpy' in the title?*
- Use flashcards or mini whiteboards to revise the following Orange letter/sound correspondences: **ce ci cy (/s/), ge (/j/), le, kn, gn, wr, tch, ea (/e/), (w)a, (/o/), y (/i/)**.
- Share and practise reading or sounding out the tricky words in this book: **today, squashed, goodbye, cupboards, precious, another, discovered, tyre, together**.
- Discuss the meaning of any unfamiliar words or phrases, such as: **grazing, airbed, snuffle, shivers ran down her back**.

Strategy check:
- Encourage the children to use phonics skills to decode any new words. If they struggle, remind them to use a range of reading strategies, e.g. saying and blending letter sounds, reading root words before endings, deciding if the text makes sense, seeing a known word or sound within a word, using picture cues and developing basic inference and deduction skills.
- Ask questions to encourage these skills, e.g. *What can you do when you come to a word that you don't know?*

DURING READING

Independent reading:
- Encourage the children to read independently while you listen to each child in the group in turn.
- Some children could read in pairs, taking turns to read a page to each other.
- Highlight examples of successful problem-solving. Say: *'Tyre' is a difficult word but you used the picture cue to help you. Well done!*
- If appropriate, pause occasionally to reread a sentence, check for understanding and discuss the illustrations. Ask: *Do you think Flora had been camping before (on page 2)? Why?*
Why do you think Mum got a bit grumpy on page 5?
Where did Flora put her socks and her duck on page 6?
Why was the bathroom floor muddy (on page 9)?
What have they bought from the shop (on page 19)?

AFTER READING

Return to the text:
- Share any words that caused difficulty with decoding, pronunciation or understanding.
- Encourage the children to reflect on their learning. Ask: *Why did Flora have a jumpy bumpy feeling when she went camping? Do you think she will want to go camping again?*
- Use the comprehension questions at the end of the book to talk about events of the story and what Flora was feeling at different points of her camping trip.
- Ask some of the following additional questions to check understanding of the book and explore the themes:
Do you think Dad and Nell will go next time? Why/why not?
Why were there cobwebs in the bathroom?
How was camping different from being at home?
Why did Mum make chocolate spread sandwiches for breakfast?

Follow-up activities:
1. Using the PCM provided, the children respond to the text and practise composition by writing a postcard from Flora to Dad and Nell. They should describe the campsite and their thoughts about camping.
2. Ask the children to write about a time when they have had a 'jumpy bumpy' feeling. It might have been a time when they were away from home. Provide words to help with spelling and ideas.
3. Set up a tent in the school grounds, if possible, to give the children the experience of what it feels like to be inside a tent. Try to replicate activities from the story, e.g. lying on an airbed in a sleeping bag, flying a kite or playing on a tyre swing.

BOOK OVERVIEW

Flora is very excited to be going on her first camping trip with Mum. Lots of things about the trip are great during the daytime, but as bedtime approaches, Flora notices how many things are different to being at home and she gets a jumpy bumpy feeling inside that won't go away. Mum comes to the rescue and helps her to see that new experiences can also be very exciting!

The Jumpy Bumpy Feeling

Name: _____ Date: _____

Write a postcard from Flora to send to Dad and Nell.
What do you think Flora would say?
Use words from the book or from the box below to help you.

To: _____
_____
_____
_____
_____
_____

Love from: _____

Dad and Nell,

25 Acorn Avenue,

Newtown

having	camping	owls hooting
time	playing	tyre swing
chocolate spread sandwich		fun
flying kites	made new friends	

Reading Planet Galaxy © Rising Stars UK Ltd 2018. You may photocopy this page.

LAUGH OUT LOUD

Orange

GUIDED GROUP READING
BEFORE READING
Book introduction:
- Look together at the cover image, title and blurb of the book. Ask: *What do you think a 'fun fact' is? Do you know any fun facts or jokes?*
- Use flashcards or mini whiteboards to revise the following Orange letter/sound correspondences: **ch (/k/), ch (/sh), ce ci (/s/), ge gi (/j/), le, mb, kn, gi, wr, tch, tion, sure (/sh/alternatives), ea (/e/), (w)a, (/o/), y (/i/)**.
- Share and practise reading or sounding out the tricky words in this book: **trampoline, gone, rhino, glorious, pizza, Naples, massive, chefs, measured, aunties, Kimani Marugue, imagine, Chana, practise, punchline**.
- Discuss the meaning of any unfamiliar words or phrases, such as: **living in the past, punchline**.

Strategy check:
- Encourage the children to use phonics skills to decode any new words. If they struggle, remind them to use a range of reading strategies, e.g. saying and blending letter sounds, reading root words before endings, deciding if the text makes sense, seeing a known word or sound within a word, using picture cues and developing basic inference and deduction skills.
- Ask questions to encourage these skills, e.g. *What can you do when you come to a word that you don't know?*

DURING READING
Independent reading:
- Encourage the children to read independently while you listen to each child in the group in turn.
- Model sounding out and blending, or ask individuals to decode words to the group.
- Discuss the purpose of the section headings.
- Highlight examples of successful problem-solving. Say: *I like the way you read ahead to predict the word 'massive'. Well done!*
- If appropriate, pause occasionally to reread a sentence, check for understanding and discuss the illustrations. Ask: *How does a quill pen work (page 2)? Why are squirrels planting trees on page 9? Why is the joke about the plumber funny (on page 11)? What do we really call the topping on the pizza on page 12?*

AFTER READING
Return to the text:
- Share any words that caused difficulty with decoding, pronunciation or understanding.
- Encourage the children to reflect on their learning. Ask: *Did the jokes make you laugh out loud? Did you find the facts fun? Say why.*
- Use the comprehension questions at the end of the book to talk about the jokes and the fun facts.
- Ask some of the following additional questions to check understanding of the book and explore the themes: *Do you know any 'Knock, knock' jokes? If you do, tell the group. Do you think everyone likes jokes? Is it easy to tell a joke? If not, explain why. Do you think it would be fun to write jokes all day? If not, why not?*

Follow-up activities:
1. Using the PCM provided, the children recall details from the book and practise writing. They fill in the gaps with the appropriate words to complete jokes from the book.
2. In your maths lesson, take a class vote to discover which are the funniest jokes in the book. You could rate jokes on a 'laughability scale' (1 to 3). Then the children can draw bar charts to illustrate your findings.

BOOK OVERVIEW
What's a duck's favourite snack? How do you make a cheese roll? The children will laugh out loud with this book packed with jokes and fun facts!

Laugh Out Loud

Name: _____ Date: _____

Fill in the gaps to complete the jokes.
Choose from the answers given below.

1. What do you call an uncle who makes you laugh?

_____

a funny uncle   a funcle   a silly uncle

2. Why did the pupil snap his pencil in half?

_____

Because it was too long.   Because it was break time.

3. What do you call a burger on roller skates?

_____

fast food   junk food   pet food

4. Why did the music teacher bring a ladder to work?

_____

So he could reach the high notes.   So he could clean the windows.

5. What is the world's saddest pizza topping?

_____

pepperoni   a Pepper-lonely   red pepper

Reading Planet Galaxy © Rising Stars UK Ltd 2018. You may photocopy this page.

Galaxy assessment guidance

The After Reading section within each guided reading session includes additional questions that can be used to challenge the children's understanding of the text. These questions are linked to National Curriculum content domain objectives and can be used to help develop comprehension. Some children may perform better when reading specific genres, for example fiction or non-fiction. So it is important that children are given opportunities to practise each objective across a range of genres to ensure that they are secure.

The Key Stage 1 English reading test focuses on the comprehension elements of the National Curriculum. The content domain outlines objectives from the Key Stage 1 National Curriculum that are assessed in the test. The table below shows the content domain objectives:

Content domain reference
1a draw on knowledge of vocabulary to understand texts
1b identify/explain key aspects of fiction and non-fiction texts, such as characters, events, titles and information
1c identify and explain the sequence of events in texts
1d make inferences from the text
1e predict what might happen on the basis of what has been read so far

The *Galaxy* monitoring and tracking grids (see pages 70–71) can be used to make notes during independent and guided group reading sessions as required. They are designed to be simple and easy to manage while providing a record of general notes and evidence of day-to-day progress.

The *Galaxy* levelled assessments (see pages 72–75) provide a more formal way to check how children are progressing within each book band. The assessments can be used at the beginning and end of a period of time to track and monitor a child's progression, for example at the beginning and end of a school term. They can also be used to check whether a child is ready to progress to the next book band or to check where a new starter should begin with the scheme.

Assessments should ideally be conducted on a one-on-one basis with the adult and child located in a comfortable, quiet space. Ensure the child does not feel pressured and explain that they are going to do a quick, fun activity to help them improve their reading.

Features of the assessments

Letters/sounds – grapheme-phoneme correspondences included at each band/level. Point to the grapheme and ask the child to say the sound.

Words – words that can be decoded at each level. Point to the word and ask the child to blend and say the word.

Pseudo words – artificial words using combinations of known letters and sounds. These prepare children for the Year 1 Phonics Screening Check and encourage them to maintain the skill of decoding unknown words. Point to the word and ask the child to blend and say the word.

Common exception words – common words that may be difficult to decode because they contain unusual letter-sound correspondences. Point to the word and ask the child to blend and say the word.

Sentences – simple sentences containing both decodable words and Common exception words. Point to the sentences and ask the child to blend the words and read the sentences.

Comprehension questions – simple retrieval questions based on the above sentences to check that the child has understood the content of the sentence. Ask the child a question about the book.

Using performance descriptors for assessment

Performance descriptors indicate what children should be achieving at various points along their educational pathway. Many schools use these as a way to compare achievement locally, regionally and nationally. With the move away from numerical level descriptors in recent years, practitioners are free to use a wider variety of tools and methods to assess children's progress.

The following approaches could be used in relation to reading:
- Use your own judgement against the curriculum objectives. For *Galaxy* Pink A to Red B the relevant curriculum objectives are the Early Learning Goals, taken from the EYFS.
- Use performance descriptors such as: 'Emerging', 'Developing', 'Secure' and 'Exceeding' to evaluate how well children are meeting the objectives.

Example of teacher assessment against ELG for reading:

Child's name: Sarah Woods	**Emerging**	**Developing**	**Secure**	**Exceeding**
Child can read and understand simple sentences.			✔	
Child can use phonics knowledge to decode regular words and read them out loud accurately.			✔	
Child can read common irregular words.		✔		
Child can demonstrate understanding when talking about what they have read.		✔		

- Use the *Galaxy* books levelled assessments as explained on page 68. This data can then be compared to previous cohorts, and teacher moderated within and across schools.
- For schools that require a more detailed approach to data analysis and tracking, *Reading Planet* is compatible with most standardised assessment packages such as *Rising Stars Progress in Reading Assessment*.

What does progress look like?

Emerging
Children working at an 'emerging' level are just beginning to demonstrate the ability to use and apply the end of year curriculum objectives. Typically, children are expected to work at an emerging level by the end of the autumn term in the child's current year group.

Developing
Children working at a 'developing' level are using and applying the end of year curriculum objectives but still with some adult support – they are not yet secure. Developing skills are expected to be displayed by the end of the spring term of the child's current year group.

Secure
Children working at a 'secure' level are able to use and apply the end-of-year curriculum objectives with confidence. Working at a secure level is the age-related expectation for the end of the summer term of the child's current year group.

Exceeding
Those children who are 'exceeding' their ability to use and apply the end-of-year curriculum objectives are demonstrating above age-expected knowledge and skills. They have surpassed the expectation for the end of the summer term of the child's current year group.

These stages can be applied to individual curriculum objectives to monitor progress closely, but are also used to form an end-of-year assessment of the child's overall attainment.

Galaxy guided group tracking and monitoring sheet

Use this tracking sheet to monitor a group's progression. A blank version of this sheet can be found on My Rising Stars.

Group/names	Book title and level	Session focus	Notes on word reading	Notes on reading for meaning	Independent or follow-on tasks
Group 1: Ella, Yasmine, Edward, Thomas	The Quack in the Kitchen	Reading with fluency, particularly when rereading	Ella – reading with fluency well. Thomas still trying to guess words from context and initial sound – move to group 2 for decoding focus?	All children able to talk confidently about what they have read. Thomas – with support	Children each wrote their own sentence related to the story topic and practised rereading to a partner to gain fluency

Reading Planet Galaxy © Rising Stars UK Ltd 2018. You may photocopy this page.

READING PLANET GALAXY

Galaxy independent tracking and monitoring sheet

Use this tracking sheet to monitor each child's progression. A blank version of this sheet can be found on My Rising Stars.

Name	Book title and level	Word reading observations	Reading for meaning observations
Thomas Taylor	Get to the Airport	Stumbling over longer words – reminded to slow down	Able to discuss meanings of words, sentences and general storyline

Galaxy Yellow reading assessment

Name:	Date:

Letters/Sounds

ar	or	ur	ure	oi	ear	air
ure	er	ar	ur	or	ow	er

Yellow words

dark	for	turn	now	start	farm	airport
picture	cow	part	rubber	forest	pointed	better

Yellow pseudo words

hort	purn	airn	fow	gark	joid	quam
cheen	dittle	uck	glipper	ture	sork	armer

Tricky words

out	some	what	when	do	were	one
said	little	like	have	so	there	come

Sentences

1	Tap glitter on top.
2	He misses his mum.
3	Mum turned into the car park.
4	The string led them down the river and into a farm.
5	She saw flowers.

Comprehension of above sentences

1	What do you tap on top?
2	Who does he miss?
3	What did Mum do?
4	Where did the string lead them?
5	What did she see?

Notes/comments

Galaxy Blue reading assessment

Name:	Date:

Letters/Sounds

wh	ay	a-e	ey	eigh	ea	ph
y	i-e	o-e	oe	ow	ie	e-e

Blue words

whisper	away	came	monkey	volcano	real	white
honey	time	home	post	snow	field	these

Blue pseudo words

clow	rinkey	hane	groe	neast	blay	grote
speal	huppy	pleme	stike	treve	bry	drowl

Tricky words

what	little	out	like	do	have	one
said	were	there	so	come	some	when

Sentences

1	The magic picture faded away.
2	The two friends sat very still.
3	They swoop low over the frozen ice and snow.
4	These cartoons were short and funny.
5	The wolf has bright red eyes and howls like a beast.

Comprehension of above sentences

1	What happened to the magic picture?
2	How many friends were there?
3	What do they swoop over?
4	Were the cartoons long?
5	What colour are the wolf's eyes?

Notes/comments

Galaxy Green reading assessment

Name:	Date:

Letters/Sounds

ew	ue	u-e	ou	ir	ere	or
our	au	ore	eer	oul	oy	oor

Green words

few	blue	tube	girl	around	toy	work
four	forever	more	first	could	there	door

Green pseudo words

thirt	muge	chere	plue	koy	nore	shor
splew	fube	azound	crole	scaw	fleer	aldue

Tricky words

oh	their	people	Mr	Mrs	looked	called
asked	could	water	where	who	again	thought

Sentences

1	A few years later their baby son was born.
2	She was going to the ballet for the first time.
3	Your skin gives you your sense of touch.
4	Around the world, flowers bloom in spring and summer.
5	He'd built something HUGE!

Comprehension of above sentences

1	When was their baby son born?
2	Had she been to the ballet before?
3	What gives you your sense of touch?
4	When do flowers bloom?
5	How big was the thing Billy had built?

Notes/comments

Galaxy Orange reading assessment

Name:	Date:

Letters/Sounds

mb	dge	ci	ture	kn	tion	ge
wr	cial	cy	gn	st	cian	tch

Orange words

cell	sign	castle	bridge	capture	knew	nation
village	icy	watch	walk	giant	wrong	head

Orange pseudo words

moticed	micy	rastle	vidge	knapter	bapture	yace
wrop	ratch	schoom	paldace	brage	pation	satch

Tricky words

could	their	where	Mr	thought	looked	who
asked	oh	water	people	called	again	Mrs

Sentences

1	The castle soldiers captured Robin and his friends.
2	He was a Samurai warrior, one of the Emperor's guards.
3	The Cyclops was a huge, wild giant with only one eye.
4	Richard decided to make flashing lights for the cattle pen.
5	Worst of all, Flora was wearing socks to keep her feet warm.

Comprehension of above sentences

1	Who captured Robin?
2	What is a Samurai warrior?
3	How many eyes did the Cyclops have?
4	What did Richard do?
5	Why was Flora wearing socks?

Notes/comments

Using a running record for assessment

A running record is a useful tool to help you analyse in closer detail how a child is accessing a text. It provides an overview of the errors, corrections and fluency with which a child is reading. Miscues can be identified and you can learn about the thinking processes the child uses.

You may use this information to:
- plan sessions that focus on the child's specific needs
- match the child to a more appropriate text
- document progression over a period of time
- group and regroup children for guided group instruction.

The child reads a short passage aloud, while the you make note of any errors, such as:
- **substitutions** – substituting an incorrect word for a word in the text
- **reversals** – reversing the order of one or two words in the text
- **insertion** – adding in a word
- **told** – words you provide to the child because they cannot read them.

If the child self-corrects after making a mistake, the word is counted correctly.

The following codes can be used to mark up the running record passage:

Behaviour	Notation	Example
Correct response	Tick above each correctly read word	✔ ✔ ✔ The children played.
Substitution	Note the substituted word above the actual word in the text	✔ ✔ **playing** The children played.
Reversal	Draw an arrow or note the response said	✔ playing children The children played.
Insertion	Use a caret and note the added word	**always** ✔ ✔ ^ ✔ The children played.
Omission	Place a dash above the word left out	✔ ✔ — The children played.
Told	Write a '**T**' above the word given	✔ ✔ T The children played.
Self-correction	Write '**SC**' above the word that has been self-corrected	✔ ✔ SC The children played.

To work out a percentage accuracy score, simply take the number of words the child has read correctly and divide it by the number of words in the passage, then multiply by 100. For example:

In a passage of 150 words, there were 12 noted errors.
150 – 12 = 138 words read correctly
138/150 = 0.92 × 100 = 92

Independent level: 95% – 100%
Instructional level: 91% – 94%
Frustration level: below 90% accuracy

Running record example

Name: Sally Jones	Date: 3rd June
Text title: Cake Time (Blue)	Text length: 50 words

Page	Text	Notes
2	✔ ✔ ✔ ✔ ✔ ✔ SC Miss Lock's class were making cakes. She ✔ ✔ ✔ ✔ ✔ — — ✔ ✔ ✔ told them to find a partner and put on an ✔ apron. ✔ ✔ ✔ Let's bake together!	
3	✔ ✔ ✔ ✔ ✔ ✔ ✔ Asha weighed the butter and sugar and ✔ ✔ ✔ ✔ ✔ ✔ T ✔ ✔ put them in a bowl. Tess asked, "Can I ✔ ✔ ✔ mix them together?"	
4	✔ ✔ ✔ ✔ ✔ ✔ ✔ ✔ Miss Lock called out, "Now crack the eggs ✔ ✔ ✔ ✔ ✔ in a jug and whisk them."	

Recording codes:
- Correct response: ✔
- Substitution: write words
- Reversal: draw arrow or write words
- Insertion: ^ add word
- Omission: —
- Told word: **T**
- Self-corrected: **SC**

Calculating percentage accuracy score:	Accuracy score:
Passage length minus errors = number of words correct 50 − 3 = 47 Number of words correct divided by passage length, times 100 = percentage score 47 / 50 = 0.94 × 100 = 94% Independent level: 95% – 100% Instructional level: 91% – 94% Frustration level: below 90% accuracy	94% Instructional level, almost independent level

Running record

Name:	Date:
Text title:	Text length:

Page	Text	Notes

Recording codes:
- Correct response: ✔
- Substitution: write words
- Reversal: draw arrow or write words
- Insertion: ^ add word
- Omission: —
- Told word: **T**
- Self-corrected: **SC**

Calculating percentage accuracy score:	**Accuracy score:**
Passage length minus errors = number of words correct Number of words correct divided by passage length, times 100 = percentage score Independent level: 95% – 100% Instructional level: 91% – 94% Frustration level: below 90% accuracy	

Rising Stars Reading Planet book banding/level chart

Band/Level	Key features	Word Count	Book length
Lilac *Reading Planet* Level 0	• Wordless books with full-page illustrations • Books provide stimulus for retelling and discussion	0	8pp
Pink A *Reading Planet* Level 1A	• One single-line sentence on every other page • Simple sentence structures and using mostly CVC words • Repetition of words and phrases • Simple, predictable text involving familiar experiences, objects and actions • Basic punctuation, including capital letters, full stops and exclamation marks • Text is fully supported by illustrations	25–35	12pp
Pink B *Reading Planet* Level 1B	As above, with the following developments: • One single-line sentence on every page • +s plural endings • Commas are introduced more regularly • Simple speech bubbles introduced	35–70	12pp
Red A *Reading Planet* Level 2A	• Slightly longer text, with one to two single-line sentences per page • Sentences are short, clear and straightforward • Simple story development • Text is fully supported by illustrations • Speech marks introduced • Simple, predicable rhyming stories are introduced	60–90	12pp
Red B *Reading Planet* Level 2B	As above, with the following developments: • Sentences can be longer than one line • Simple labels, sub-headings and captions (non-fiction) • -es plural endings	90–120	12pp
Yellow *Reading Planet* Level 3	• Wider range of sentence structure and print location on the page • Some repetition of vocabulary, phrases and ideas • More episodes introduced in storylines • More fantastical/imaginary events • Characters are slightly more developed • -ing, -ed, -er, -est endings	120–200	16pp
Blue *Reading Planet* Level 4	• Wider range of sentence structures and content • Increased mix of natural and literary language • Similar-looking words call for an element of word-solving (e.g. the/then) • Further development of characters and scope for making predictions about actions and events • Artwork supports text rather than directly conveying meaning • Contractions and alternative verbs for speech are introduced	200–300	16pp
Green *Reading Planet* Level 5	• Content includes a larger number of characters and events • More sophisticated humour, suspense and prediction opportunities (fiction) • More specialised vocabulary (non-fiction) • Varied placement of text and images • Simple fact boxes and a wider range of text types (non-fiction)	300–450	20pp
Orange *Reading Planet* Level 6	• Sentence structures become more developed • Readers should be able to infer meaning from the text • Overall meaning of text is supported by artwork • Italics are used for emphasis	450–550	20pp
Turquoise *Reading Planet* Level 7	• More developed episodes and events with longer descriptions • Increased use of literary language • Greater variation in dialogue • Non-fiction texts contain longer, more formal sentences • Graphs, maps and diagrams often included (non-fiction) • Wider range of punctuation	550–700	24pp
Purple *Reading Planet* Level 8	• Storylines are more involved • Simple subtexts and themes are introduced • Some books may have short chapters (fiction) • Stories convey more of the writer's personal feelings • More opportunities for readers to discuss characters and their motivations	600–800	24pp
Gold *Reading Planet* Level 9	• More complex sentence structures • Characters are more distinct and developed • Non-fiction can include charts, diagrams and glossaries	800–1000	24pp
White *Reading Planet* Level 10	• Longer sentence structures with more subordinate clauses and literary language • More implied information including more metaphorical expressions • All fiction books have short chapters • Texts are placed in a broader context and include more detailed information (non-fiction) • An increased amount of specialist vocabulary is included (non-fiction)	1200–1400	32pp

Discover more from Rising Stars Reading Planet

Lift-off

Beautiful wordless books to get every child reading-ready

Give every child a solid base to begin their reading journey and prepare for phonics and word reading with this Lift-off wordless books. Children will develop the essential early language skills needed through beautifully illustrated and engaging books featuring speech rhythm activities.

What's available:
- 12 paired Lift-off wordless books for Lilac
- 1 Teacher's Guide
- 6 colourful posters
- Audio recordings with songs, music, rhymes and sound-effects for each book

Lift-off First Words

Bridge the gap between wordless books and first reading books

Support very early readers as they transition from wordless books to initial decoding with Lift-off First Words. This unique strand of Lilac band books feature a single word or short phrase per double-page to support children as they practise their emerging reading skills through blending and segmenting Phase 1 and 2 words.

What's available:
- 12 paired fiction and non-fiction First Words books for Lilac
- 1 Teacher's Guide
- 6 colourful posters
- Audio recordings with songs, music, rhymes and sound-effects for each book

Rocket Phonics

Fully decodable phonics books to support progress in word reading and comprehension

Help children develop a strong foundation in word reading, and practise their decoding skills with Rocket Phonics. These fresh and modern phonics reading books are perfect for young readers to consolidate their learning and begin to develop their comprehension skills.

What's available:
- 72 fully decodable reading books for Pink A to Orange
- 3 Teacher's Guides
- Audio narratives for each book

COMING JANUARY 2019 24 readers 1 Teacher's Guide

Comet Street Kids

A modern character series to engage all readers

Support every child in becoming a confident and independent reader through the action-packed adventures of Rav, Finn, Asha, Tess and Stefan. These expertly levelled reading books, feature diverse characters and modern stories that will captivate children and breathe new life into early reading for teachers and parents.

What's available:
- 144 reading books for Pink A to White
- 6 Teacher's Guides
- Audio narratives for each book

www.risingstarsreadingplanet.com